Beyond Instant Noodles. 200 Quick & Easy College Recipes:

Simple, Budget-Friendly Meals for Students

Copyright © 2023 Javier Sanz
ISBN: 9798871165188
All rights reserved

Thank you!

So, we went a little crazy and put together this monster cookbook with 200 recipes from all over the world. Why? Because we remember those days of being stuck between the same old cafeteria food and instant noodles. Dark times, my friends.

Parents, if you're reading this - your kids are gonna think you're the coolest for hooking them up. Students, get ready to become the most popular person on your floor. (Pro tip: Food is the ultimate friend-maker.)

If this book saves you from another night of sad microwave meals, spread the love! Drop a review on Amazon. Your stories might just inspire another poor soul to put down the instant ramen and pick up a spatula.

Now go forth and cook something awesome! Your taste buds (and future self) will thank you.

☆☆☆☆☆

You can use this QR code to submit your review

TABLE OF CONTENTS

BREAKFAST ... 10

Classic Pancakes ... 11
Shakshuka ... 12
Spanish Tortilla ... 13
Overnight Oats ... 14
Smoothie Bowl ... 15
English Breakfast ... 16
Quinoa Breakfast Bowl ... 18
Avocado Toast ... 19
Pan Con Tomate ... 20

APPETIZERS ... 21

Bruschetta ... 22
Spinach and Artichoke Dip ... 23
Guacamole ... 24
Shrimp Cocktail ... 25
Caprese Salad ... 26
Mini Quiches ... 27
Sweet Potato Fries ... 29
Ceviche ... 30
Buffalo Cauliflower Bites ... 31

SALADS ... 32

Caesar Salad ... 33
Greek Salad ... 35
Waldorf Salad ... 34
Cobb Salad ... 36
Panzanella ... 37
Asian Noodle Salad ... 38
Beet and Goat Cheese Salad ... 39
Watermelon Feta Salad ... 40
Roasted Vegetable Salad ... 41
Coleslaw ... 42

SOUPS ... 43

Chicken Noodle Soup 44

Minestrone 45

Gazpacho 46

Potato Leek Soup 47

Lentil Soup 48

Miso Soup 49

Cream of Mushroom 50

Tomato Basil Soup 51

Butternut Squash Soup 52

Clam Chowder 53

MAINS - MEAT 54

Spaghetti Carbonara 55

Beef Stroganoff 56

Chicken Marsala 57

Coq au Vin 59

Pork Chops with Apple Sauce 61

Lamb Chops with Mint Jelly 62

Tandoori Chicken 63

BBQ Ribs 64

Beef Bourguignon 65

Chicken Alfredo 66

MAINS - SEAFOOD 67

Shrimp Scampi 69

Lobster Thermidor 70

Tuna Steak 71

Fish and Chips 72

Cioppino 73

Clam Linguine 74

Paella 75

Crab Cakes 76

Sushi Rolls 77

MAINS - VEGETARIAN 78

Ratatouille 80

Vegetable Stir-Fry 81

Cauliflower Steak 82
Lentil Curry 83
Stuffed Bell Peppers.. 84
Sweet Potato Curry 85
Chickpea salad... 86
Vegan Tacos 87
Mushroom Risotto 88

SIDES 89

Garlic Bread.. 90
Mashed Potatoes 91
Grilled Asparagus 92
Rice Pilaf 93
Roasted Brussels Sprouts.. 94
Quinoa Salad 95
Mac and Cheese 96
Seasoned roasted sweet potatoes 98
Greek Tzatziki 99

BREADS 100

Sourdough Bread.. 101
Focaccia.. 102
Baguette 103
Ciabatta 104
Cornbread 105
Banana Bread.. 106
Pumpkin Bread 107
Brioche 108
Challah... 109
Pita Bread 110

PASTA 111

Penne Arrabbiata.. 112
Fettuccine Alfredo 113
Pesto Linguine 114
Spaghetti Bolognese 115
Lasagna.. 116

Tortellini Soup 117
Aglio e Olio... 118
Pasta Primavera 119
Lobster Ravioli 120
Gnocchi 121

DESSERTS..122

Chocolate Cake..123
Apple Pie 124
Cheesecake 125
Panna Cotta 126
Chocolate Chip Cookies................................127
Brownies 128
Tiramisu...129
Santiago Cake 130
S'mores 131
Rice Pudding 132

BEVERAGES...133

Margarita...134
Lemonade 135
Smoothies 136
Kalimotxo...137
Milkshake 138
Mimosa..139
Hot Chocolate 140
Mojito 141
Piña Colada 142
Moscow Mule..143

SAUCES AND DIPS..144

Marinara Sauce..145
Pesto Sauce 146
Tzatziki Sauce..147
Easy Aioli 148
Romesco 149
Salsa Brava 150

Salsa Verde 151
Barbecue Sauce 152
Honey Mustard 153
Roasted Red Pepper Sauce 154

SNACKS 155

Trail Mix 156
Homemade Popcorn 157
Veggie Chips 158
Chocolate-Covered Strawberries 159
Cheese Sticks 160
Rice Krispies Treats 161
Pretzels 162
Granola Bars 163
Mixed Nuts 164
Pistachio Granola 165

ASIAN CUISINE 166

Pad Thai 167
Sushi 168
Spring Rolls 169
Teriyaki Chicken 170
Miso Ramen 171
Bao Buns 172
Dumplings 173
Kung Pao Chicken 174
Tempura 175
Korean Beef and Rice 176

EUROPEAN CUISINE 177

Shepherd's Pie 178
French Onion Soup 179
Pulpo a la Gallega 180
Osso Buco 181
salmorejo 182
Gambas al ajillo 183
Moussaka 184

Goulash 185
Huevos Rotos 186
Chateaubriand 187

MIDDLE EASTERN CUISINE 188

Hummus 190
Falafel.. 191
Kofta 192
Tabouleh..193
Baba Ganoush.......................................194
Lamb meatballs.....................................195
Lamb Tagine 196
Kebabs 197
Baklava 198

LATIN CUISINE 199

Reina Pepiada 200
Empanadas 201
Cubano Sandwich.................................202
Arepas 203
Tamales...204
Churros 205
Chimichurri..206
Pupusas...207
Mole 208
Feijoada 209

FESTIVE AND HOLIDAY 210

Roast Turkey 211
Glazed Ham...212
Pumpkin Pie 213
Fruitcake 214
Holiday Cookies 215
Eggnog 216
Latkes 217
Hot Cross Buns 218
Corned Beef and Cabbage 219

Beef Wellington 220

QUICK AND EASY 222

Chicken Stir-Fry 223
California BLT 224
Apple Tarts 225
Garlic Mushroom 226
Sheet Pan Fajitas 227
Grilled Cheese Sandwich 228
Chocolate Mousse 229
Breakfast Burrito...230
Mason Jar Salad 231
Microwave Mug Cake 232

Breakfast

Breakfast

CLASSIC PANCAKES

INGREDIENTS:

1 1/2 CUPS ALL-PURPOSE FLOUR
3 1/2 TSP BAKING POWDER
1/2 TSP SALT
1 TBSP SUGAR
1 1/4 CUPS MILK
1 EGG
3 TBSP UNSALTED BUTTER, MELTED

RECIPE:

1. In a bowl, combine the dry ingredients: flour, baking powder, salt and sugar.
2. Make a well in the center and pour in the milk, egg, and melted butter. Mix until just incorporated.
3. Heat a lightly oiled saucepan over medium-high heat. Pour the batter into the pan. The ratio should be ~ 1/4 cup per pancake. Brown on both sides and serve hot.

Fun Fact: The world's largest pancake was made in England and had a diameter of 49 feet and 3 inches!

Chef Insight: For fluffy pancakes, mix just until the dry ingredients are moistened. Be cautious about overmixing—it results in flat, chewy pancakes. A few lumps are okay.

SHAKSHUKA

INGREDIENTS:

1 TABLESPOON OLIVE OIL
1 ONION, CHOPPED
1 BELL PEPPER, CHOPPED
2 CLOVES GARLIC, MINCED
1 CAN (14 OZ) CRUSHED TOMATOES
1 TEASPOON PAPRIKA
1 TEASPOON CUMIN
4-6 EGGS
SALT AND PEPPER TO TASTE

RECIPE:

1. Heat olive oil in a skillet over medium heat.
2. Sauté onion, bell pepper, and garlic until softened.
3. Add crushed tomatoes, paprika, and cumin. Simmer for 10 minutes.
4. Make wells in the sauce and crack an egg into each well.
5. Cover and cook until eggs are done to your liking.

Fun Fact: Shakshuka originally comes from North Africa and is especially popular in Tunisian, Libyan, Algerian, and Moroccan cuisines.

Chef Insight: The eggs are the star here; keep an eye on them. You want the whites set but the yolk still runny for that classic shakshuka experience.

Breakfast

SPANISH TORTILLA

INGREDIENTS:

4-5 MEDIUM POTATOES, PEELED AND THINLY SLICED
1 MEDIUM ONION, THINLY SLICED
6-8 LARGE EGGS
1 CUP OLIVE OIL
SALT TO TASTE

RECIPE:

1. Heat the olive oil in a non-stick skillet over medium heat. Add the potato slices and onion. Cook until tender but not browned.
2. Drain the potatoes and onions, reserving the olive oil.
3. In a bowl, beat the eggs and add salt to taste.
4. Gently mix the cooked potatoes and onions into the beaten eggs.
5. Heat 2 tablespoons of the reserved olive oil in the same skillet over medium heat.
6. Pour the potato-egg mixture into the skillet.
7. Cook for about 4-5 minutes, or until the bottom is lightly golden.
8. Flip the tortilla using a large plate and cook the other side for another 4-5 minutes.

Fun Fact: The Spanish Tortilla has nothing to do with the Mexican flatbread of the same name. It's more like a frittata and is popular in tapas bars across Spain.

Chef Insight: The key to a great tortilla is the slow cooking of the potatoes and onions. They should practically melt into the eggs.

OVERNIGHT OATS

INGREDIENTS:

1 CUP OLD-FASHIONED OATS
1 CUP MILK (DAIRY OR NON-DAIRY)
1/2 CUP GREEK YOGURT
1 TABLESPOON CHIA SEEDS
(OPTIONAL)
1 TABLESPOON HONEY OR MAPLE

SYRUP
1/2 TEASPOON VANILLA EXTRACT
1/2 CUP FRUIT (E.G., BERRIES,
BANANA SLICES)
ADDITIONAL TOPPINGS: NUTS, SEEDS,
OR COCONUT FLAKES

RECIPE:

1. In a mason jar or airtight container, add the old-fashioned oats.
2. Pour in the milk and Greek yogurt.
3. Add chia seeds, if using.
4. Drizzle in the honey or maple syrup for sweetness.
5. Add the vanilla extract for flavor.
6. Stir to combine everything, ensuring the oats are submerged.
7. Seal the container and place it in the refrigerator overnight.
8. In the morning, give the oats a good stir. If they're too thick, add a little more milk to reach your desired consistency.
9. Top with fresh fruit and any additional toppings you like

Fun Fact: Oats are a great source of fiber, particularly beta-glucan, which is known for its ability to lower cholesterol.

Chef Insights: You can get creative with your overnight oats by using different types of milk, sweeteners, and toppings. Almond milk and coconut milk are excellent non-dairy options, while a dollop of almond or peanut butter can add a nutty richness to the dish.

Breakfast

SMOOTHIE BOWL

INGREDIENTS:

1 FROZEN BANANA
1/2 CUP FROZEN BERRIES
1/2 CUP COCONUT MILK
TOPPINGS: GRANOLA, NUTS, SEEDS, FRESH FRUITS

RECIPE:

1. Blend the frozen banana, frozen berries, and coconut milk until smooth.
2. Pour into a bowl and decorate with your choice of toppings.

Fun Fact: The smoothie bowl trend started to take off around 2016 and became a popular way to make smoothies more substantial and visually appealing.

Chef Insight: Choose a variety of textures for your toppings to make each bite interesting. Think crunchy granola, chewy dried fruits, and creamy nut butter. The secret to a thick smoothie bowl is using frozen fruits. Resist the urge to add too much liquid; you want a thick consistency to hold all your toppings.

ENGLISH BREAKFAST

INGREDIENTS:

2 SAUSAGES
2 STRIPS OF BACON
2 EGGS
1 TOMATO, HALVED
1 CUP BAKED BEANS
2 SLICES OF TOAST
1 CUP BUTTON MUSHROOMS, SLICED

RECIPE:

1. In a large skillet, cook sausages and bacon until browned. Set aside and keep warm.
2. In the same skillet, cook the tomato halves and mushrooms until softened.
3. Meanwhile, heat baked beans in a separate pan.
4. Fry or poach the eggs to your liking.
5. Serve everything hot with slices of toast.

Fun Fact: The full English breakfast is also known colloquially as a "fry-up" in the UK.

Chef Insight: For a more authentic experience, you can add black pudding and hash browns to the platter. Timing is everything. Start with the components that take longest to cook (like sausages) and work your way down to a hot and ready plate.

Breakfast

MATCHA SMOOTHIE

INGREDIENTS:

1 FROZEN BANANA
1 CUP ALMOND MILK
1 TEASPOON MATCHA POWDER
1 TABLESPOON HONEY OR AGAVE SYRUP
ICE CUBES (OPTIONAL)

RECIPE:

1. Blend all the ingredients until smooth.
2. Serve immediately, over ice if desired.

Fun Fact: Matcha is a type of powdered green tea that originated in China but became an integral part of the Japanese tea ceremony.

Chef Insight: The quality of matcha can greatly affect the taste. Ceremonial-grade matcha is the highest quality and will offer a more vibrant color and smoother flavor. Make sure to sift your matcha powder before blending to avoid any lumps. Quality matcha makes a difference.

QUINOA BREAKFAST BOWL

INGREDIENTS:

1 CUP COOKED QUINOA
1/2 CUP ALMOND MILK
1/2 CUP FRESH BERRIES
1 TABLESPOON CHIA SEEDS
1 TABLESPOON HONEY OR MAPLE SYRUP

RECIPE:

1. Heat the cooked quinoa and almond milk in a pot over low heat until warm.
2. Transfer to a bowl and top with fresh berries, chia seeds, and sweetener of your choice.

Fun Fact: Although often referred to as a grain, quinoa is actually a seed from a plant called goosefoot, which is related to spinach and beets.

Chef Insight: Rinse quinoa thoroughly before cooking to remove its natural coating of saponins, which can make it taste bitter or soapy. The sky is the limit for toppings. Go seasonal for fresh, local flavors.

Breakfast

AVOCADO TOAST

INGREDIENTS:

2 SLICES OF WHOLE-GRAIN BREAD
1 RIPE AVOCADO
1 EGG
1 TEASPOON OLIVE OIL
SALT AND PEPPER TO TASTE
OPTIONAL TOPPINGS: RADISH SLICES, MICROGREENS,
RED PEPPER FLAKES

RECIPE:

1. Cut the avocado in half, and scoop the flesh into a bowl.
2. Mash the avocado with a fork and mix in olive oil. Season with salt and pepper.
3. Toast the slices of bread until golden and crispy.
4. Fry/poach an egg. You want the whites set but the yolk still runny. The mix between the yolk and the salty avocado is sublime.
5. Assemble. Spread the mashed avocado onto the toasted bread, with the egg on top.
6. Add any optional toppings like radish slices, microgreens, or red pepper flakes

Fun Fact: Avocado toast became a massive food trend in the 2010s. Avocados contain two times more potassium than bananas.

Chef's Tip: You can add some lime or lemon juice to not only add flavor, but also to help keep the avocado from browning quickly.

PAN CON TOMATE

INGREDIENTS:

1 BAGUETTE, SLICED DIAGONALLY INTO 1/2-INCH PIECES
2-3 RIPE TOMATOES, HALVED
2 CLOVES OF GARLIC, PEELED
EXTRA VIRGIN OLIVE OIL
SALT TO TASTE

RECIPE:

1. Grill or toast the baguette slices until they are crispy and golden brown.
2. While the bread is still hot, rub one side of each slice with a garlic clove. The garlic will melt into the bread, infusing it with flavor.
3. Rub the same side of the bread with the cut side of a tomato half. Press slightly to ensure the bread absorbs the tomato juices. You can also blend the tomato and then spread it.
4. Drizzle a generous amount of extra virgin olive oil over the tomato-rubbed side of the bread.
5. Sprinkle with salt to taste.

Fun Fact: Pan con Tomate is often served with jamón serrano or Manchego cheese in Spain.

Chef Insight: The quality of your tomatoes and olive oil will make a significant difference in this dish. Choose ripe, flavorful tomatoes and a good-quality extra virgin olive oil for the best results.

Appetizers

Appetizers

BRUSCHETTA

INGREDIENTS:

1 BAGUETTE, SLICED
4 RIPE TOMATOES, DICED
1 CLOVE GARLIC, MINCED
2 TABLESPOONS OLIVE OIL
2 TABLESPOONS BALSAMIC VINEGAR
8 BASIL LEAVES, CHIFFONADE
SALT AND PEPPER TO TASTE

RECIPE:

1. Preheat oven to 350°F (175°C).
2. Place baguette slices on a baking sheet and toast for 8 minutes.
3. In a mixing bowl, combine tomatoes, garlic, olive oil, balsamic vinegar, and basil.
4. Spoon the mixture onto toasted baguette slices, then season with salt and pepper.

Fun Fact: Bruschetta actually refers to the grilled bread, not the topping. The dish originated from 15th-century Italy! By the way, it's pronounced /broo-skeh-tuh/

Chef Insight: Use a serrated knife to cut your tomatoes. It's less likely to crush them, keeping all those beautiful juices in the fruit where they belong.

SPINACH AND ARTICHOKE DIP

INGREDIENTS:

1 (10-OUNCE) PACKAGE FROZEN CHOPPED SPINACH, THAWED AND DRAINED
1 (14-OUNCE) CAN ARTICHOKE HEARTS, DRAINED AND CHOPPED
1/2 CUP MAYONNAISE
1/2 CUP SOUR CREAM
1 CUP GRATED PARMESAN CHEESE
1 TEASPOON MINCED GARLIC
1/4 TEASPOON CRUSHED RED PEPPER FLAKES (OPTIONAL)
SALT AND BLACK PEPPER TO TASTE
1 CUP SHREDDED MOZZARELLA CHEESE

RECIPE:

1. Preheat your oven to 375°F (190°C).
2. In a mixing bowl, combine the chopped spinach, chopped artichoke hearts, mayonnaise, sour cream, and grated Parmesan.
3. Add the minced garlic and crushed red pepper flakes, if using.
4. Season with salt and black pepper to taste. Mix ingredients.
5. Transfer the mixture to a greased baking dish and top with shredded mozzarella cheese.
6. Bake for 25-30', or until the dip is bubbly and the top is golden.
7. Serve warm with your choice of dippers like tortilla chips, sliced baguette, or vegetable sticks.

Fun Fact: Artichokes are one of the oldest cultivated vegetables. Greeks and Romans loved their purported health benefits.

Chef Insights: For an even creamier texture, you can add a package of cream cheese to the mix. If you're looking to make it a bit lighter, you can opt for low-fat versions of sour cream.

Appetizers

GUACAMOLE

INGREDIENTS:

3 RIPE AVOCADOS
1 SMALL WHITE ONION, FINELY CHOPPED
1/2 CUP CILANTRO, FINELY CHOPPED
1 GARLIC CLOVE, MINCED
1 LIME, JUICED
1 TEASPOON SALT

RECIPE:

1. Mash avocados in a bowl.
2. Add all other ingredients adjusting for salt until perfect flavor
3. Mix until smooth and serve immediately.

Fun Fact: Avocados are technically berries. Yes, you heard that right!

Chef Insight: Always make guacamole as close to serving time as possible to prevent it from browning. Adding lime juice not only adds flavor but also helps keep the color vibrant. Fold in some finely chopped jalapeños for a spicy kick. Traditional guacamole does not contain tomatoes, but feel free to add them in small cubes.

SHRIMP COCKTAIL

INGREDIENTS:

1 LB LARGE SHRIMP, PEELED AND DEVEINED
1 CUP COCKTAIL SAUCE
1 LEMON, QUARTERED

RECIPE:

1. Bring a pot of salted water to a boil.
2. Add shrimp and cook until pink, about 2-3 minutes.
3. Drain and immediately transfer to an ice bath.
4. Serve chilled with cocktail sauce and lemon wedges.

Fun Fact: Shrimp turn pink when cooked due to a heat-sensitive pigment called astaxanthin.

Chef Insight: For an elegant presentation, hang the shrimp on the rim of a martini or margarita glass filled with cocktail sauce. Also, consider making your own cocktail sauce with ketchup, horseradish, and a splash of Worcestershire sauce. It's all about the details.

Appetizers

CAPRESE SALAD

INGREDIENTS:

4 RIPE TOMATOES, SLICED
1 LB FRESH MOZZARELLA, SLICED
1 BUNCH FRESH BASIL
2 TABLESPOONS OLIVE OIL
2 TABLESPOONS BALSAMIC REDUCTION
SALT AND PEPPER TO TASTE

RECIPE:

1. Alternate tomato slices, mozzarella slices, and basil leaves on a platter.
2. Drizzle with olive oil and balsamic reduction.
3. Season with salt and pepper.

Fun Fact: Caprese salad comes from the island of Capri in Italy.

Chef Insight: opt for a high-quality extra virgin olive oil and aged balsamic vinegar. The ingredients are simple, so make them count. You can try balsamic reduction instead of balsamic vinegar for a sweeter, more concentrated flavor and a beautiful glaze-like finish.

MINI QUICHES

INGREDIENTS:

1 READY-MADE PIE CRUST
4 EGGS
1 CUP MILK
1 CUP SHREDDED CHEESE (YOUR CHOICE)
1/2 CUP DICED VEGETABLES (E.G., BELL PEPPERS, SPINACH)
SALT AND PEPPER TO TASTE

RECIPE:

1. Preheat oven to 375°F (190°C).
2. Cut pie crust into small circles and press them into a mini muffin tin.
3. In a bowl, whisk together eggs, milk, cheese, vegetables, salt, and pepper.
4. Fill each mini crust with the egg mixture.
5. Bake for 20 minutes or until set.

Fun Fact: Quiche is believed to have originated in Germany, not France as commonly thought.

Chef Insight: Feel free to get creative with the fillings. A good quiche is like a blank canvas, open to endless culinary possibilities. Smoked salmon, sautéed mushrooms, or even a touch of truffle oil can take these to a whole new level.

Appetizers

CHEESE BOARD

INGREDIENTS:

ASSORTED CHEESES (HARD, SOFT, AND BLUE)
ASSORTED CRACKERS AND BREAD
FRESH AND DRIED FRUITS
NUTS
HONEY OR PRESERVES

RECIPE:

1. Arrange: Place cheeses at varying points on a board.
2. Fill In the gaps: Add crackers, bread, fruits, and nuts around the cheese.
3. Final Touch: Drizzle some honey or add a small bowl of preserves.

Fun Fact: The oldest known cheese was found in an Egyptian tomb and is over 4,000 years old.

Chef Insight: Offer a variety of textures and flavors on your cheese board. Include a mix of creamy, crumbly, sweet, and savory to keep the palate intrigued. Include a cheese knife for each type of cheese. Pairing each cheese with a specific cracker or fruit will elevate the experience.

SWEET POTATO FRIES

INGREDIENTS:

2 LARGE SWEET POTATOES, PEELED AND CUT INTO FRIES
2 TABLESPOONS OLIVE OIL
1 TEASPOON PAPRIKA
1 TEASPOON GARLIC POWDER
SALT AND PEPPER TO TASTE

RECIPE:

1. Preheat your oven to 400°F (200°C) and line a baking sheet with parchment paper.
2. In a large bowl, toss the sweet potato fries with olive oil, paprika, and garlic powder.
3. Arrange the fries in a single layer on the baking sheet.
4. Bake for 30-35 minutes, turning halfway through, until crispy and golden.

Fun Fact: Sweet potatoes are not actually potatoes; they belong to the morning glory family.

Chef Insight: The key to crispy sweet potato fries is spacing them well apart on the baking sheet. Overcrowding leads to steaming, which means less crispiness. A dusting of grated Parmesan in the last 5 minutes of baking adds a rich, salty component.

Appetizers

CEVICHE

INGREDIENTS:

1 LB FRESH, FIRM WHITE FISH (E.G., TILAPIA, SEA BASS), DICED
1 CUP FRESH LIME JUICE
1 RED ONION, THINLY SLICED
1 JALAPEÑO, SEEDED AND MINCED
1/2 CUP CILANTRO, CHOPPED
SALT TO TASTE

RECIPE:

1. In a glass bowl, combine fish and lime juice, ensuring the fish is fully submerged.
2. Cover and refrigerate for at least 4 hours, or until the fish turns opaque.
3. Drain most of the lime juice, leaving a little to keep the dish moist.
4. Add onion, jalapeño, cilantro, and salt. Mix gently and serve immediately.

Fun Fact: Ceviche is thought to have originated in Peru more than 2,000 years ago.

Chef Insight: The acid in the lime juice "cooks" the fish without heat. Always use fresh, high-quality fish, and keep it chilled for food safety.

BUFFALO CAULIFLOWER BITES

INGREDIENTS:

1 HEAD CAULIFLOWER, CUT INTO FLORETS
1 CUP ALL-PURPOSE FLOUR
1 CUP MILK OR PLANT-BASED MILK
1/2 CUP BUFFALO SAUCE
1 TEASPOON GARLIC POWDER
SALT AND PEPPER TO TASTE

RECIPE:

1. Preheat the oven to 450°F (230°C). Line a baking sheet with parchment paper.
2. In a bowl, whisk together the flour, milk, garlic powder, salt, and pepper.
3. Dip each cauliflower floret into the batter, ensuring it's well-coated.
4. Place the coated florets on the baking sheet and bake for 20 minutes.
5. Remove from the oven, toss with buffalo sauce, and bake for another 10 minutes.

Fun Fact: Cauliflower comes in multiple colors including white, green, purple, and orange.

Chef Insight: For a healthier twist, try using an air fryer for the cauliflower bites. They'll be just as crispy but with less oil.

Salads

CAESAR SALAD

INGREDIENTS:

1 HEAD OF ROMAINE LETTUCE, WASHED AND TORN INTO BITE-SIZE PIECES
1 CUP CROUTONS
1/2 CUP PARMESAN CHEESE, GRATED
2 CLOVES GARLIC, MINCED
1 TEASPOON ANCHOVY PASTE OR 2 WHOLE ANCHOVIES, MINCED (OPTIONAL)
1/2 CUP MAYONNAISE
2 TABLESPOONS LEMON JUICE
1 TEASPOON DIJON MUSTARD
SALT AND BLACK PEPPER TO TASTE

RECIPE:

1. In a large bowl, combine the romaine lettuce, croutons, and half of the grated Parmesan cheese.
2. In a separate bowl, mix together the garlic, anchovy paste (if using), mayonnaise, lemon juice, and Dijon mustard. Whisk until smooth.
3. Season the dressing with salt and black pepper to your liking.
4. Just before serving, toss the salad with the dressing until well coated.
5. Sprinkle the remaining Parmesan cheese on top for garnish.

Fun Fact: Caesar Salad was not named for Julius Caesar as some might think. The dish was created in 1924 by Caesar Cardini, an Italian-American restaurateur.

Chef Insights: Freshly grated Parmesan cheese will provide a much better flavor than pre-grated versions. If you're making your own croutons, consider adding some garlic powder or Italian seasoning for extra flair.

Salads

WALDORF SALAD

INGREDIENTS:

3 LARGE APPLES, CORED AND DICED
1 CUP WALNUTS, COARSELY
CHOPPED
1 CUP CELERY, THINLY SLICED
1/2 CUP MAYONNAISE

1 TABLESPOON LEMON JUICE
SALT AND BLACK PEPPER TO TASTE
LETTUCE LEAVES, FOR SERVING
OPTIONAL: 1/2 CUP SEEDLESS
GRAPES, HALVED

RECIPE:

1. In a large mixing bowl, combine the diced apples, chopped walnuts, and sliced celery.
2. In a separate small bowl, whisk together the mayonnaise and lemon juice.
3. Pour the dressing over the apple mixture.
4. Season with salt and black pepper to taste.
5. Toss everything together until well coated.
6. If you're using grapes, fold them into the salad.
7. Serve on a bed of lettuce leaves.

Fun Fact: The original Waldorf Salad was much simpler, containing only apples, celery, and mayonnaise. Walnuts and other ingredients like grapes were added in later versions of the recipe.

Chef Insights: To add more complexity to the flavors, you can toast the walnuts before adding them to the salad. If you're not a fan of mayonnaise, try substituting it with yogurt for a lighter and tangier version.

GREEK SALAD

INGREDIENTS:

3 LARGE RIPE TOMATOES, CUT INTO WEDGES
1 CUCUMBER, SLICED INTO HALF-MOONS
1 GREEN BELL PEPPER, SLICED
1 RED ONION, THINLY SLICED

1/2 CUP KALAMATA OLIVES
1 BLOCK OF FETA CHEESE (200G)
1/4 CUP EXTRA-VIRGIN OLIVE OIL
1 TEASPOON DRIED OREGANO
JUICE OF 1 LEMON
SALT AND PEPPER TO TASTE

RECIPE:

1. In a large bowl, combine the tomatoes, cucumber, green bell pepper, and red onion.
2. Add the Kalamata olives to the mixture.
3. Place the block of feta cheese on top of the vegetables.
4. In a separate small bowl, whisk together the olive oil, oregano, lemon juice, salt, and pepper.
5. Drizzle the dressing over the salad covering the feta cheese.
6. Serve immediately, or let it sit for a few minutes to allow the flavors to meld together.

Fun Fact: Did you know that in Greece, this salad is often enjoyed as a complete meal and not just a side dish? It's a testament to how satisfying and hearty this simple mixture of fresh ingredients can be.

Chef Insights: Use a quality extra-virgin olive oil for the best flavor. For an authentic touch, don't crumble the feta. Keep it in a large block or slice and place it on top. You can also add a few capers for an extra burst of flavor.

Salads

COBB SALAD

INGREDIENTS:

4 CUPS MIXED SALAD GREENS
1 CUP GRILLED CHICKEN, CHOPPED
1 AVOCADO, SLICED
1 CUP CHERRY TOMATOES, HALVED

1/2 CUP BLUE CHEESE, CRUMBLED
2 HARD-BOILED EGGS, SLICED
4 SLICES BACON, COOKED AND
CRUMBLED

FOR THE DRESSING:

1/2 CUP OLIVE OIL
3 TABLESPOONS RED WINE VINEGAR
1 TEASPOON DIJON MUSTARD
SALT AND PEPPER TO TASTE

RECIPE:

1. Arrange the salad greens on a platter.
2. Neatly arrange the chicken, avocado, tomatoes, blue cheese, eggs, and bacon on top.
3. Whisk together the dressing ingredients and drizzle over the salad.

Fun Fact: The Cobb Salad was invented at the Hollywood Brown Derby restaurant and is named after the restaurant's owner, Robert Howard Cobb.

Chef Insight: You can personalize this salad by using your favorite ingredients. The key is to have a variety of textures and flavors.

PANZANELLA

INGREDIENTS:

4 CUPS STALE BREAD CUBES
4 LARGE TOMATOES, CHOPPED
1 CUCUMBER, SLICED
1 RED ONION, THINLY SLICED
1 BUNCH BASIL LEAVES, TORN

FOR THE DRESSING:

1/4 CUP OLIVE OIL
2 TABLESPOONS BALSAMIC VINEGAR
SALT AND PEPPER TO TASTE

RECIPE:

1. In a large bowl, combine bread, tomatoes, cucumber, onion, and basil.
2. Whisk together the dressing ingredients and pour over the salad. Toss to combine.
3. Let the salad sit for at least 30 minutes to allow flavors to meld.

Fun Fact: Panzanella is a Tuscan dish traditionally made in the summer with ripe tomatoes and stale bread.

Chef Insight: Don't rush this one—the bread needs time to soak up the juicy goodness from the vegetables and dressing.

Salads

ASIAN NOODLE SALAD

INGREDIENTS:

4 CUPS COOKED SOBA NOODLES
1 CUP SHREDDED CARROTS
1 RED BELL PEPPER, THINLY SLICED
1 CUCUMBER, JULIENNED

1 BUNCH GREEN ONIONS, CHOPPED
1/4 CUP CHOPPED CILANTRO
1/4 CUP CHOPPED PEANUTS

FOR THE DRESSING:

1/4 CUP SOY SAUCE
2 TABLESPOONS RICE VINEGAR
1 TABLESPOON SESAME OIL
1 TABLESPOON PEANUT BUTTER
1 TEASPOON GRATED GINGER
1 CLOVE GARLIC, MINCED

RECIPE:

1. Combine the soba noodles, carrots, bell pepper, cucumber, green onions, and cilantro in a large bowl.
2. Whisk together the dressing ingredients until smooth. Pour over the salad and toss.
3. Garnish with chopped peanuts before serving.

Fun Fact: Soba noodles are made from buckwheat flour and are a staple in Japanese cuisine.

Chef Insight: Feel free to customize with your preferred protein like grilled chicken or tofu for a heartier meal.

BEET AND GOAT CHEESE SALAD

INGREDIENTS:

4 MEDIUM BEETS, ROASTED AND PEELED
4 CUPS ARUGULA
1/2 CUP GOAT CHEESE, CRUMBLED
1/4 CUP TOASTED WALNUTS

FOR THE DRESSING:

1/4 CUP OLIVE OIL
2 TABLESPOONS BALSAMIC VINEGAR
SALT AND PEPPER TO TASTE

RECIPE:

1. Slice the roasted beets and arrange them over the arugula on a serving platter.
2. Sprinkle with crumbled goat cheese and toasted walnuts.
3. Whisk together the dressing ingredients and drizzle over the salad.

Fun Fact: Beets are a great source of antioxidants and give a beautiful color to the dish.

Chef Insight: Use gloves when handling beets to avoid staining your hands.

Salads

WATERMELON FETA SALAD

INGREDIENTS:

4 CUPS CUBED WATERMELON,
SEEDLESS
1 CUP FETA CHEESE, CRUMBLED
1/2 CUP FRESH MINT LEAVES,
FINELY CHOPPED

1/4 CUP RED ONION, THINLY SLICED
2 TBSP OLIVE OIL
1 TBSP BALSAMIC GLAZE
SALT AND PEPPER TO TASTE

RECIPE:

1. Place the cubed watermelon in a large bowl.
2. Add the crumbled feta cheese and thinly sliced red onion.
3. Sprinkle the finely chopped fresh mint leaves over the ingredients.
4. Drizzle olive oil and balsamic glaze over the salad.
5. Toss gently to combine all ingredients.
6. Season with salt and pepper to taste.
7. Serve immediately or chill for a short time before serving.

Fun Fact: Watermelons are 92% water, which makes them an excellent hydrating food, especially during hot summer days.

Chef Insights: Balsamic glaze adds a sweet, tangy finish, but you can also use a dash of lime juice for a more zesty flavor. Make sure to serve this salad soon after making it, as watermelon tends to release water over time and can make the salad a bit soggy.

ROASTED VEGETABLE SALAD

INGREDIENTS:

4 CUPS MIXED VEGETABLES (BELL PEPPERS, ZUCCHINI, CARROTS), DICED
2 TABLESPOONS OLIVE OIL
SALT AND PEPPER TO TASTE

FOR THE DRESSING:

1/4 CUP OLIVE OIL
2 TABLESPOONS BALSAMIC VINEGAR
1 CLOVE GARLIC, MINCED
SALT AND PEPPER TO TASTE

RECIPE:

1. Preheat the oven to 400°F (200°C). Toss the vegetables in olive oil, salt, and pepper.
2. Spread the vegetables on a baking sheet and roast for 20-25 minutes, until tender.
3. Allow the vegetables to cool slightly, then place them in a large bowl.
4. Whisk together the dressing ingredients and pour over the roasted vegetables. Toss to combine.

Fun Fact: Roasting vegetables caramelizes their natural sugars, offering a unique, smoky sweetness.

Chef Insight: Feel free to include seasonal vegetables or your personal favorites for a customized dish.

Salads

COLESLAW

INGREDIENTS:

4 CUPS SHREDDED CABBAGE
1 CUP SHREDDED CARROTS
1/2 CUP MAYONNAISE
2 TABLESPOONS APPLE CIDER VINEGAR
1 TABLESPOON SUGAR
SALT AND PEPPER TO TASTE

RECIPE:

1. In a large bowl, combine shredded cabbage and carrots.
2. In a separate bowl, mix mayonnaise, apple cider vinegar, sugar, salt, and pepper.
3. Pour the dressing over the cabbage mixture and toss until well-coated.

Fun Fact: The term "coleslaw" comes from the Dutch word "koolsla," meaning "cabbage salad."

Chef Insight: You can add your twist to this classic dish by adding ingredients like chopped apples, raisins, or even a dash of hot sauce for some heat.

Soups

Soups

CHICKEN NOODLE SOUP

INGREDIENTS:

1 WHOLE CHICKEN (ABOUT 3-4 POUNDS), CUT INTO PIECES
8 CUPS OF WATER
2 CARROTS, PEELED AND SLICED
2 CELERY STALKS, SLICED
1 LARGE ONION, CHOPPED
2 GARLIC CLOVES, MINCED

1 TEASPOON THYME
1 TEASPOON ROSEMARY
2 BAY LEAVES
2 CUPS EGG NOODLES
SALT AND PEPPER TO TASTE
OPTIONAL: CHOPPED PARSLEY FOR GARNISH

RECIPE:

1. Place the chicken pieces in a pot and cover with 8 cups of water.
2. Bring to a boil, then reduce the heat to low and simmer for about 1 hour, or until the chicken is tender.
3. Remove the chicken pieces from the broth and set aside to cool. Strain the broth and return it to the pot.
4. Add vegetables and herbs to the broth.
5. Bring the mixture to a boil, then reduce the heat and simmer until the vegetables are tender, about 20 minutes.
6. In the meantime, remove the chicken meat from the bones and shred it into bite-sized pieces.
7. Add the chicken and egg noodles to the pot. Cook until the noodles are tender, about 10 minutes.
8. Season with salt and pepper to taste. Optional: Garnish with chopped parsley before serving.

Fun Fact: Did you know that chicken soup has been a recommended remedy for illness since ancient times?

Chef Insights: For a deeper flavor, try roasting the chicken and vegetables before adding them to the broth.

MINESTRONE

INGREDIENTS:

4 CUPS VEGETABLE BROTH
1 CUP DICED TOMATOES
1 CUP DICED ZUCCHINI
1 CUP CANNELLINI BEANS
1/2 CUP DICED ONIONS
1/2 CUP DICED CARROTS
1/2 CUP ELBOW PASTA

RECIPE:

1. In a large pot, sauté onions and carrots until soft.
2. Add the vegetable broth and bring to a simmer.
3. Stir in tomatoes, zucchini, and cannellini beans.
4. Add the pasta and cook until al dente.
5. Season with salt, pepper, and a sprinkle of Parmesan cheese if desired.

Fun Fact: Minestrone varies by region in Italy; the ingredients can depend on the vegetables that are in season.

Chef Insight: A splash of good quality olive oil before serving enhances the overall flavor profile.

Soups

GAZPACHO

INGREDIENTS:

6 RIPE TOMATOES, CHOPPED
1 CUCUMBER, PEELED AND CHOPPED
1 BELL PEPPER, CHOPPED
1 SMALL RED ONION, CHOPPED
3 CUPS TOMATO JUICE
3 GARLIC CLOVES, MINCED

1/4 CUP OLIVE OIL
3 TABLESPOONS RED WINE VINEGAR
SALT AND PEPPER TO TASTE
FRESH BASIL OR PARSLEY FOR
GARNISH

RECIPE:

1. In a blender or food processor, add the chopped tomatoes, cucumber, bell pepper, red onion, and garlic.
2. Pulse until the vegetables are finely chopped but not pureed.
3. Transfer the mixture to a large bowl and add the tomato juice, olive oil, and red wine vinegar.
4. Mix well and season with salt and pepper.
5. Chill the soup in the refrigerator for at least 2 hours.
6. Serve cold, garnished with fresh basil or parsley.

Fun Fact: Gazpacho has ancient roots, and the original version is believed to have included stale bread, olive oil, and water, pounded in a mortar. Tomatoes and peppers were added only after they were brought to Spain from the New World.

Chef Insights: For the most flavorful gazpacho, use ripe, in-season tomatoes. If you prefer a smoother texture, you can puree half the vegetable mixture and leave the other half chunky for varied texture. Some people like to add a drizzle of balsamic glaze just before serving for extra oomph.

POTATO LEEK SOUP

INGREDIENTS:

4 CUPS CHICKEN OR VEGETABLE BROTH
2 LARGE POTATOES, DICED
2 LEEKS, CLEANED AND SLICED
1 CUP HEAVY CREAM
2 TABLESPOONS BUTTER

RECIPE:

1. Melt butter in a pot and sauté the leeks until soft.
2. Add the diced potatoes and broth, and bring to a simmer.
3. Cook until potatoes are tender, then blend until smooth.
4. Stir in the heavy cream and season with salt and pepper to taste.

Fun Fact: Leeks are part of the onion family but have a milder, sweeter flavor.

Chef Insight: You can garnish with crispy bacon bits or chives for an extra layer of flavor.

Soups

LENTIL SOUP

INGREDIENTS:

4 CUPS VEGETABLE BROTH
1 CUP GREEN LENTILS
1 CUP DICED CARROTS
1 CUP DICED CELERY
1 ONION, CHOPPED
2 CLOVES GARLIC, MINCED

RECIPE:

1. Sauté the onion and garlic until fragrant.
2. Add the lentils, carrots, and celery, and pour in the vegetable broth.
3. Simmer until lentils are tender, then season with salt and pepper.

Fun Fact: Lentils are a great source of plant-based protein and are very versatile.

Chef Insight: For a smoky flavor, consider adding a dash of smoked paprika.

MISO SOUP

INGREDIENTS:

4 CUPS DASHI (JAPANESE FISH STOCK)
3 TABLESPOONS MISO PASTE
1 CUP TOFU, CUBED
1 CUP SEAWEED, SLICED
2 GREEN ONIONS, CHOPPED

RECIPE:

1. Bring the dashi to a simmer in a pot.
2. Dissolve the miso paste in a small amount of hot dashi and add it back to the pot.
3. Add tofu and seaweed and simmer until heated through.
4. Garnish with green onions before serving.

Fun Fact: Miso is a traditional Japanese seasoning made by fermenting soybeans with salt and koji.

Chef Insight: Don't boil the miso, as it can kill the beneficial probiotics and alter the flavor.

Soups

CREAM OF MUSHROOM

INGREDIENTS:

4 CUPS CHICKEN OR VEGETABLE BROTH
2 CUPS SLICED MUSHROOMS
1 CUP HEAVY CREAM
1 ONION, DICED
2 CLOVES GARLIC, MINCED
2 TABLESPOONS BUTTER

RECIPE:

1. Sauté the onions and garlic in butter until translucent.
2. Add mushrooms and cook until soft.
3. Pour in the broth and bring to a simmer.
4. Blend the soup until smooth and then return to the pot.
5. Stir in the heavy cream and season with salt and pepper.

Fun Fact: Mushrooms are packed with nutrients and have been used for their medicinal properties for centuries.

Chef Insight: Use a variety of mushrooms for a more complex flavor—like a combination of cremini, shiitake, and portobello.

TOMATO BASIL SOUP

INGREDIENTS:

4 CUPS CHICKEN OR VEGETABLE BROTH
4 CUPS DICED TOMATOES
1 CUP FRESH BASIL LEAVES
1 ONION, DICED
2 CLOVES GARLIC, MINCED
2 TABLESPOONS OLIVE OIL

RECIPE:

1. Sauté onions and garlic in olive oil until soft.
2. Add tomatoes and broth and bring to a simmer.
3. Add basil leaves and simmer for 10 minutes.
4. Blend the soup until smooth and season with salt and pepper.

Fun Fact: Basil is often considered the king of herbs and is native to India.

Chef Insight: For a creamier texture, you can add a splash of heavy cream after blending.

Soups

BUTTERNUT SQUASH SOUP

INGREDIENTS:

4 CUPS CHICKEN OR VEGETABLE BROTH
1 BUTTERNUT SQUASH, PEELED AND CUBED
1 ONION, DICED
1 APPLE, PEELED AND CHOPPED
2 CLOVES GARLIC, MINCED
2 TABLESPOONS OLIVE OIL

RECIPE:

1. Sauté onions and garlic in olive oil.
2. Add squash, apple, and broth, then bring to a simmer.
3. Cook until squash is tender, then blend until smooth.
4. Season with salt, pepper, and a dash of nutmeg.

Fun Fact: Butternut squash is rich in fiber, vitamins, and minerals.

Chef Insight: Roasting the squash before adding it to the soup can deepen the flavors.

Beyond Instant Noodles. 200 Quick & Easy College Recipes

CLAM CHOWDER

INGREDIENTS:

4 CUPS CLAM JUICE OR FISH STOCK
1 CUP CHOPPED CLAMS
2 CUPS DICED POTATOES
1 CUP DICED ONIONS
1 CUP HEAVY CREAM
2 TABLESPOONS BUTTER

RECIPE:

1. Melt butter and sauté onions until soft.
2. Add potatoes and clam juice and bring to a simmer.
3. Cook until potatoes are tender, then add the clams.
4. Stir in the heavy cream and simmer for an additional 5 minutes.

Fun Fact: Clam chowder is a popular dish in coastal regions and has various regional adaptations.

Chef Insight: Use fresh clams for the best flavor but be careful not to overcook them, as they can become rubbery.

Mains

—

Meat

SPAGHETTI CARBONARA

INGREDIENTS:

400G SPAGHETTI
4 LARGE EGGS
1 CUP PECORINO ROMANO CHEESE, GRATED
1 CUP PARMESAN CHEESE, GRATED

200G GUANCIALE OR PANCETTA, DICED
FRESHLY GROUND BLACK PEPPER
SALT TO TASTE
A PINCH OF PARSLEY FOR GARNISH

RECIPE:

1. Cook the spaghetti in a large pot of salted boiling water until al dente. Drain, reserving 1 cup of pasta water.
2. In a separate bowl, whisk together the eggs, Pecorino Romano, Parmesan, and a good amount of freshly ground black pepper.
3. In a large skillet, cook the guanciale or pancetta over medium heat until it becomes crispy. Remove from heat and set aside.
4. Add the drained spaghetti to the skillet with the cooked guanciale. Toss to coat the pasta in the fat.
5. Remove the skillet from heat and quickly mix in the egg and cheese mixture, stirring quickly to avoid scrambling the eggs. Add reserved pasta water a tablespoon at a time to achieve desired consistency.
6. Serve immediately with additional grated Pecorino Romano and black pepper. Garnish with parsley if you like.

Fun Fact: Authentic Carbonara has no cream! Many variations exist, but the original Roman recipe relies solely on the emulsion created by pasta water, cheese, and eggs for its creamy texture.

Chef Insights: It's crucial to mix in the egg and cheese mixture off the heat. This ensures you don't get scrambled eggs.

BEEF STROGANOFF

INGREDIENTS:

1.5 LBS BEEF SIRLOIN OR TENDERLOIN, SLICED INTO STRIPS
2 TABLESPOONS OLIVE OIL
1 ONION, FINELY CHOPPED
1 LB MUSHROOMS, SLICED
2 CLOVES GARLIC, MINCED
1 CUP BEEF BROTH
1 TABLESPOON WORCESTERSHIRE SAUCE
1 CUP SOUR CREAM
SALT AND PEPPER TO TASTE
FRESH PARSLEY, FOR GARNISH
COOKED EGG NOODLES OR RICE, FOR SERVING

RECIPE:

1. Heat olive oil in a large skillet over medium-high heat. Add beef strips and cook until browned. Remove beef from the skillet and set aside.
2. In the same skillet, add chopped onion and sauté until translucent. Add garlic and mushrooms, cooking until mushrooms have softened.
3. Add beef broth and Worcestershire sauce, stirring to combine. Lower the heat and let the sauce simmer for about 10 minutes.
4. Add the sour cream to the skillet, stirring until well combined. Return the beef to the skillet and cook until heated through.
5. Season with salt and pepper to taste. Garnish with fresh parsley.
6. Serve over cooked egg noodles or rice.

Fun Fact: Beef Stroganoff was named after Count Pavel Stroganov, a 19th-century Russian noble. The dish was likely his chef's creation, and it won a cooking contest in 1891.

Chef Insights: For maximum tenderness, slice the beef against the grain. You can also add a splash of white wine for extra flavor.

CHICKEN MARSALA

INGREDIENTS:

4 BONELESS, SKINLESS CHICKEN BREASTS
1 CUP ALL-PURPOSE FLOUR, FOR DREDGING
SALT AND FRESHLY GROUND BLACK PEPPER
4 TABLESPOONS OLIVE OIL

1 LB CREMINI OR WHITE MUSHROOMS, SLICED
1 CUP MARSALA WINE
1 CUP CHICKEN BROTH
2 TABLESPOONS UNSALTED BUTTER
2 TABLESPOONS FRESH PARSLEY, CHOPPED

RECIPE:

1. Pound the chicken breasts to even 1/2-inch thickness. Mix flour, salt, and black pepper on a plate, and dredge each chicken breast in the mixture.
2. Heat olive oil in a large skillet over medium-high heat. Add the chicken and cook until brown, about 5 minutes per side. Remove chicken and set aside.
3. In the same skillet, add mushrooms and sauté until brown and juices have been released, about 5 minutes.
4. Add the Marsala wine and bring to a boil. Scrape the brown bits from the pan and add the chicken broth. Return the chicken to the pan and simmer for 10 minutes, until it is cooked through.
5. Remove the chicken and set aside. Add butter and cook until it has fully incorporated into the sauce. Return the chicken to the skillet, turning to coat in the sauce.
6. Sprinkle with chopped parsley before serving.

Fun Fact: Marsala wine was initially fortified with alcohol to ensure that it would last on long sea voyages. Today, it adds a deep, rich flavor to dishes like Chicken Marsala that's hard to replicate.

Chef Insights: Dredging the chicken in flour helps to give it a slightly crispy texture, which contrasts wonderfully with the soft mushrooms and silky sauce. Use a good quality Marsala wine that you would drink, not a "cooking Marsala." This dish is best served immediately but can be reheated gently if needed. Pair it with a simple pasta or potato dish to make a complete meal.

COQ AU VIN

INGREDIENTS:

4 CHICKEN THIGHS AND 4
DRUMSTICKS (OR A WHOLE CHICKEN,
CUT INTO 8 PIECES)
4 OZ BACON, DICED
1 BOTTLE OF RED WINE (750ML)
2 CUPS CHICKEN STOCK
2 ONIONS, DICED
2 CARROTS, DICED
8 OZ MUSHROOMS, SLICED

4 CLOVES GARLIC, MINCED
3 SPRIGS FRESH THYME
2 BAY LEAVES
SALT AND PEPPER TO TASTE
2 TABLESPOONS OLIVE OIL
2 TABLESPOONS FLOUR
2 TABLESPOONS BUTTER
FRESH PARSLEY FOR GARNISH

RECIPE:

1. In a large pot or Dutch oven, sauté bacon until crisp. Remove bacon, leaving fat in the pot.
2. Season the chicken pieces with salt and pepper. Brown them in the bacon fat over medium-high heat. Remove and set aside.
3. Add the onions, carrots, and garlic to the pot. Sauté until onions are translucent.
4. Sprinkle flour over the vegetables and stir well to combine.
5. Deglaze the pot with red wine, scraping any bits from the bottom. Add chicken stock, thyme, and bay leaves.
6. Return the chicken and bacon to the pot. Bring to a simmer and cook, covered, for 45 minutes to an hour.
7. In a separate pan, sauté mushrooms in butter until browned. Add them to the pot.
8. Continue to simmer for another 10 minutes. Check seasoning and adjust if necessary.
9. Garnish with fresh parsley before serving.

Fun Fact: In traditional recipes, an older rooster was often used for this dish, requiring a longer cooking time to tenderize the meat. Nowadays, we often use chicken, which is more tender and cooks faster.

Chef Insights: Use a good quality wine that you would actually drink. The flavor will concentrate as it cooks. You can make this dish a day ahead. In fact, it often tastes better the next day! If you want to add an extra layer of flavor, marinate the chicken pieces in red wine overnight before cooking.

Beyond Instant Noodles. 200 Quick & Easy College Recipes

PORK CHOPS WITH APPLE SAUCE

INGREDIENTS:

4 PORK CHOPS
2 APPLES, PEELED AND DICED
1 CUP APPLE CIDER
1 TEASPOON CINNAMON
2 TABLESPOONS OLIVE OIL

RECIPE:

1. Sauté the apples in a pan until softened.
2. Add apple cider and cinnamon, and cook until it becomes a sauce.
3. Season pork chops and cook in olive oil until browned and cooked through.
4. Serve the pork chops with the apple sauce.

Fun Fact: Apples and pork have a long-standing culinary partnership, celebrated in many cultures.

Chef Insight: Choose tart apples like Granny Smith for a more balanced apple sauce.

Mains - Meat

LAMB CHOPS WITH MINT JELLY

INGREDIENTS:

4 LAMB CHOPS
1 CUP MINT LEAVES
1/2 CUP SUGAR
1/2 CUP APPLE CIDER VINEGAR
2 TABLESPOONS OLIVE OIL

RECIPE:

1. In a pot, combine mint leaves, sugar, and vinegar. Simmer until it forms a jelly-like consistency.
2. Season lamb chops and cook in olive oil until desired doneness.
3. Serve lamb chops with the mint jelly.

Fun Fact: Mint has been used as a culinary herb for thousands of years.

Chef Insight: Mint jelly cuts through the richness of the lamb, providing a refreshing counterpoint.

TANDOORI CHICKEN

INGREDIENTS:

4 CHICKEN LEG QUARTERS
1 CUP YOGURT
2 TABLESPOONS TANDOORI MASALA
1 TABLESPOON LEMON JUICE
1 TEASPOON TURMERIC
SALT TO TASTE

RECIPE:

1. Mix yogurt, tandoori masala, lemon juice, turmeric, and salt.
2. Marinate the chicken in this mixture for at least 2 hours, preferably overnight.
3. Grill the chicken until fully cooked, turning occasionally for even cooking.

Fun Fact: Tandoori cooking originated in the Indian subcontinent and uses a clay oven called a tandoor.

Chef Insight: If you don't have a tandoor, you can also use an oven's broiler setting to mimic the high heat.

Mains - Meat

BBQ RIBS

INGREDIENTS:

2 RACKS OF PORK RIBS
2 CUPS BBQ SAUCE
1 TABLESPOON PAPRIKA
1 TABLESPOON GARLIC POWDER
SALT AND PEPPER TO TASTE

RECIPE:

1. Season the ribs with paprika, garlic powder, salt, and pepper.
2. Bake in the oven at 300°F (150°C) for 2-3 hours until tender.
3. Slather with BBQ sauce and finish on the grill for a smoky flavor.

Fun Fact: Barbecue styles differ vastly across regions, particularly in the United States.

Chef Insight: Slow cooking the ribs in the oven before grilling ensures they're tender and juicy.

BEEF BOURGUIGNON

INGREDIENTS:

2 LBS BEEF CHUCK, CUBED
1 BOTTLE RED WINE
1 ONION, DICED
2 CUPS MUSHROOMS, SLICED
2 CLOVES GARLIC, MINCED
2 TABLESPOONS OLIVE OIL

RECIPE:

1. Brown the beef cubes in olive oil and set aside.
2. Sauté the onions, garlic, and mushrooms in the same pan.
3. Return the beef to the pan and add red wine.
4. Simmer until the beef is tender and the wine has reduced into a sauce.

Fun Fact: This dish originated in Burgundy, France, and traditionally uses wine from the region.

Chef Insight: Using a wine you'd enjoy drinking makes a significant difference in the dish's depth of flavor.

Mains - Meat

CHICKEN ALFREDO

INGREDIENTS:

4 BONELESS CHICKEN BREASTS
4 CUPS FETTUCCINE PASTA
2 CUPS HEAVY CREAM
1 CUP GRATED PARMESAN CHEESE
2 TABLESPOONS OLIVE OIL
SALT AND PEPPER TO TASTE

RECIPE:

1. Cook fettuccine pasta in boiling salted water until al dente.
2. In a separate pan, season and cook chicken breasts in olive oil until fully cooked.
3. In a saucepan, bring heavy cream to a simmer and add grated Parmesan.
4. Combine pasta, chicken, and Alfredo sauce, mixing well.

Fun Fact: Although Alfredo sauce feels Italian, it's more of an Italian-American creation.

Chef Insight: Freshly grated Parmesan melts more smoothly than pre-grated, giving you a creamier Alfredo sauce.

Mains

—

Seafood

Mains - Seafood

GRILLED SALMON

INGREDIENTS:

4 (6-OUNCE) SALMON FILLETS
1/4 CUP OLIVE OIL
1/4 CUP LEMON JUICE
3 CLOVES GARLIC, MINCED
1 TEASPOON DRIED OREGANO

1 TEASPOON DRIED THYME
SALT AND PEPPER TO TASTE
LEMON WEDGES AND FRESH DILL,
FOR GARNISH

RECIPE:

1. In a bowl, mix together olive oil, lemon juice, garlic, oregano, and thyme.
2. Place salmon fillets in a shallow dish and pour the marinade over them. Cover and refrigerate for at least 30 minutes, up to 2h.
3. Preheat your grill to medium-high heat. Oil the grill grates to prevent sticking.
4. Remove the salmon from the marinade and season both sides with salt and pepper.
5. Grill the salmon for about 4-5 minutes per side, or until the fish flakes easily with a fork.
6. Garnish with lemon wedges and fresh dill before serving.

Fun Fact: Did you know that salmon is one of the few foods naturally rich in vitamin D? That's a big plus, especially for those who have limited exposure to sunlight.

Chef Insights: If you're using skin-on salmon, grilling skin-side down makes for easier flipping and keeps the fish moist. Avoid over-marinating the salmon, as the acid from the lemon juice can start to "cook" the fish.

SHRIMP SCAMPI

INGREDIENTS:

1 LB LARGE SHRIMP, PEELED AND DEVEINED
4 CLOVES GARLIC, MINCED
1/4 CUP WHITE WINE
4 TABLESPOONS BUTTER
JUICE OF 1 LEMON

RECIPE:

1. Sauté the garlic in butter until fragrant.
2. Add the shrimp and cook until pink.
3. Deglaze the pan with white wine and add lemon juice.
4. Serve over pasta or with crusty bread.

Fun Fact: "Scampi" originally referred to a type of lobster. The dish has evolved to primarily use shrimp.

Chef Insight: Quality shrimp make or break this simple dish—opt for fresh, large shrimp for the best result.

Mains - Seafood

LOBSTER THERMIDOR

INGREDIENTS:

2 WHOLE LOBSTERS, HALVED
2 CUPS BÉCHAMEL SAUCE
1 CUP GRUYÈRE CHEESE, GRATED
2 TABLESPOONS BRANDY
2 TABLESPOONS MUSTARD

RECIPE:

1. Preheat your oven to 400°F (200°C).
2. Remove the meat from the lobster shells and chop into chunks.
3. Mix the lobster meat with béchamel sauce, brandy, and mustard.
4. Fill the empty lobster shells with the mixture.
5. Top with grated Gruyère and bake until golden.

Fun Fact: The dish was named after the 1891 operetta "Thermidor" by Victorien Sardou.

Chef Insight: This dish is rich—every ingredient should be of the highest quality to achieve the perfect balance.

Beyond Instant Noodles. 200 Quick & Easy College Recipes

TUNA STEAK

INGREDIENTS:

4 TUNA STEAKS
1/4 CUP SOY SAUCE
2 TABLESPOONS SESAME OIL
1 TABLESPOON GINGER, MINCED
1 TABLESPOON GARLIC, MINCED

RECIPE:

1. Mix soy sauce, sesame oil, ginger, and garlic to create a marinade.
2. Marinate the tuna steaks for at least 30 minutes.
3. Sear on high heat for 1-2 minutes on each side, depending on thickness and desired doneness.

Fun Fact: Tuna is one of the most widely consumed fish globally and has a rich history in Japanese cuisine.

Chef Insight: Always opt for sushi-grade tuna when you're cooking it to medium-rare or rare.

Mains - Seafood

FISH AND CHIPS

INGREDIENTS:

4 WHITE FISH FILLETS (SUCH AS COD OR HADDOCK)
2 CUPS FLOUR
1 BOTTLE BEER
4 LARGE POTATOES, CUT INTO FRIES
VEGETABLE OIL FOR FRYING

RECIPE:

1. Make a beer batter by mixing flour and beer.
2. Heat oil to 375°F (190°C).
3. Dip fish fillets in the batter and fry until golden brown.
4. Fry the potato cuts until golden and crispy.

Fun Fact: Fish and Chips became popular in the UK in the 19th century and quickly became a staple.

Chef Insight: Using beer in the batter makes it light and crispy, offering a delightful contrast to the flaky fish inside.

CIOPPINO

INGREDIENTS:

1 LB MIXED SEAFOOD (SHRIMP, SCALLOPS, MUSSELS)
1 CAN CRUSHED TOMATOES
1 ONION, CHOPPED
3 CLOVES GARLIC, MINCED
1 CUP WHITE WINE
2 CUPS FISH STOCK

RECIPE:

1. Sauté onion and garlic in olive oil until translucent.
2. Add crushed tomatoes, white wine, and fish stock. Bring to a simmer.
3. Add the seafood and cook until done.

Fun Fact: Cioppino is an Italian-American dish originating from San Francisco.

Chef Insight: Don't overcook the seafood—each type should be added based on its cooking time to keep everything tender.

Mains - Seafood

CLAM LINGUINE

INGREDIENTS:

1 LB LINGUINE
2 DOZEN CLAMS
4 CLOVES GARLIC, MINCED
1/4 CUP WHITE WINE
2 TABLESPOONS OLIVE OIL
CHOPPED PARSLEY FOR GARNISH

RECIPE:

1. Cook linguine al dente in salted boiling water.
2. Sauté garlic in olive oil.
3. Add clams and white wine. Cover and steam until clams open.
4. Toss in the cooked linguine and garnish with parsley.

Fun Fact: Linguine means "little tongues" in Italian, likely referring to its long, flat shape.

Chef Insight: Fresh clams make all the difference. Discard any that don't open after cooking, as they might be bad.

PAELLA

INGREDIENTS:

2 CUPS ARBORIO RICE
1 LB CHICKEN, CUT INTO PIECES
1 LB MIXED SEAFOOD (SHRIMP, MUSSELS, SQUID)
1 RED BELL PEPPER, SLICED
1 ONION, DICED
1 TEASPOON SAFFRON THREADS
4 CUPS CHICKEN STOCK

RECIPE:

1. In a paella pan, sauté onion and bell pepper until soft.
2. Add chicken pieces and brown on all sides.
3. Stir in rice and saffron threads.
4. Pour in chicken stock and simmer until rice is almost cooked.
5. Add the mixed seafood and cook until done.

Fun Fact: Paella originated in Valencia, Spain, and was traditionally cooked over open flames.

Chef Insight: Saffron is key for authentic paella. It gives the dish its characteristic color and flavor.

Mains - Seafood

CRAB CAKES

INGREDIENTS:

1 LB LUMP CRABMEAT
1/2 CUP BREADCRUMBS
1 EGG, BEATEN
2 TABLESPOONS MAYONNAISE
1 TEASPOON OLD BAY SEASONING
2 TABLESPOONS PARSLEY, CHOPPED

RECIPE:

1. Mix crabmeat, breadcrumbs, egg, mayonnaise, Old Bay, and parsley.
2. Form into patties.
3. Pan-fry in a little oil until each side is golden brown.

Fun Fact: Crab cakes are a staple in American seafood cuisine, particularly in the Mid-Atlantic and New England.

Chef Insight: Using lump crabmeat provides a meaty texture, making for more satisfying crab cakes.

SUSHI ROLLS

INGREDIENTS:

2 CUPS SUSHI RICE, COOKED AND SEASONED
1 LB SUSHI-GRADE FISH (SALMON, TUNA)
1 AVOCADO, SLICED
1 CUCUMBER, JULIENNED
NORI SHEETS
SOY SAUCE FOR DIPPING

RECIPE:

1. Place a nori sheet on a bamboo rolling mat covered with plastic wrap.
2. Spread a thin layer of rice over the nori.
3. Lay your choice of fish, avocado, and cucumber across the center.
4. Roll tightly using the bamboo mat, then slice into pieces.
5. Serve with soy sauce.

Fun Fact: Sushi dates back to ancient times and was originally a way to preserve fish in fermented rice.

Chef Insight: The quality of the rice and the freshness of the fish are crucial for outstanding sushi. Always use sushi-grade fish for safety and taste.

Mains

—

Vegetarian

EGGPLANT PARMESAN

INGREDIENTS:

2 LARGE EGGPLANTS, SLICED 1/2-INCH THICK
3 CUPS MARINARA SAUCE
2 CUPS SHREDDED MOZZARELLA CHEESE
1 CUP GRATED PARMESAN CHEESE
2 CUPS BREADCRUMBS

3 LARGE EGGS
1 CUP ALL-PURPOSE FLOUR
1/2 CUP FRESH BASIL LEAVES, FOR GARNISH
SALT AND PEPPER TO TASTE
OLIVE OIL, FOR FRYING

RECIPE:

1. Preheat the oven to 375°F (190°C).
2. Sprinkle salt on the eggplant slices and let them sit for 30 minutes to draw out moisture. Pat dry with paper towels.
3. Beat eggs in a shallow bowl. Place flour and breadcrumbs in separate shallow bowls.
4. Heat olive oil in a skillet over medium heat. Dredge each eggplant slice in flour, dip in egg, and coat with breadcrumbs. Fry each slice until golden brown, about 2-3 minutes per side. Drain on paper towels.
5. In a baking dish, spread a layer of marinara sauce. Place layers of eggplant slices, followed by mozzarella and Parmesan.
6. Bake for 25-30 minutes, or until bubbly and golden. Garnish with fresh basil before serving.

Fun Fact: Did you know that eggplant is actually a fruit, not a vegetable? Like tomatoes and peppers.

Chef Insights: Salting the eggplant not only helps to remove excess moisture but also helps to eliminate any bitterness.

Mains - Vegetarian

RATATOUILLE

INGREDIENTS:

1 EGGPLANT, DICED
1 ZUCCHINI, DICED
1 BELL PEPPER, DICED
1 ONION, DICED
1 CAN CRUSHED TOMATOES
2 CLOVES GARLIC, MINCED
THYME AND ROSEMARY TO TASTE

RECIPE:

1. Sauté each vegetable separately until slightly softened.
2. Combine in a large pot, add crushed tomatoes, garlic, and herbs.
3. Simmer until all vegetables are tender.

Fun Fact: Ratatouille comes from the Occitan "ratatolha" and first appeared in French cuisine in the late 18th century.

Chef Insight: Cooking each vegetable separately ensures they each maintain their unique texture and flavor.

Beyond Instant Noodles. 200 Quick & Easy College Recipes

VEGETABLE STIR-FRY

INGREDIENTS:

2 CUPS MIXED VEGETABLES (BELL PEPPERS, CARROTS, BROCCOLI)
1/4 CUP SOY SAUCE
2 TABLESPOONS SESAME OIL
1 TABLESPOON GINGER, MINCED
2 CLOVES GARLIC, MINCED

RECIPE:

1. Heat a wok or large skillet over high heat.
2. Add sesame oil, ginger, and garlic.
3. Stir-fry the vegetables until crisp-tender.
4. Add soy sauce and toss to coat.

Fun Fact: Stir-frying is a Chinese cooking technique that dates back to the Ming Dynasty.

Chef Insight: High heat and quick cooking are key; this locks in the flavors and nutrients of the vegetables.

Mains - Vegetarian

CAULIFLOWER STEAK

INGREDIENTS:

1 LARGE CAULIFLOWER
1/4 CUP OLIVE OIL
2 CLOVES GARLIC, MINCED
1 TEASPOON SMOKED PAPRIKA
SALT AND PEPPER TO TASTE

RECIPE:

1. Cut the cauliflower into thick "steaks."
2. Mix olive oil, garlic, smoked paprika, salt, and pepper.
3. Brush the mixture onto both sides of the cauliflower steaks.
4. Grill or roast at 400°F (200°C) until tender and slightly charred

Fun Fact: Cauliflower is a cruciferous vegetable, a family that also includes broccoli, Brussels sprouts, and cabbage.

Chef Insight: Roasting or grilling cauliflower brings out its natural nuttiness and sweetness.

LENTIL CURRY

INGREDIENTS:

1 CUP LENTILS, WASHED AND DRAINED
1 LARGE ONION, FINELY CHOPPED
1 LARGE TOMATO, DICED
1 CAN COCONUT MILK (400ML)
2 CLOVES GARLIC, MINCED
1-INCH GINGER, GRATED
1 TEASPOON TURMERIC POWDER
1 TEASPOON CUMIN SEEDS
1 TEASPOON CORIANDER POWDER
1 TEASPOON CHILI POWDER (ADJUST TO TASTE)
2 TABLESPOONS VEGETABLE OIL
SALT TO TASTE
FRESH CILANTRO LEAVES, FOR GARNISH

RECIPE:

1. Heat oil in a large pot over medium heat. Add cumin seeds and let them sizzle for a few seconds.
2. Add chopped onions and sauté until translucent.
3. Stir in the garlic and ginger, cooking until fragrant.
4. Add in all the spices (turmeric, coriander, and chili powder) and sauté for another minute.
5. Add tomatoes and cook until they break down into a sauce.
6. Add lentils, coconut milk, and 2 cups of water. Bring to a boil.
7. Reduce heat to low, cover, and simmer for 30-40 minutes, or until lentils are tender. Stir occasionally to prevent sticking.
8. Adjust seasoning and garnish with fresh cilantro leaves.

Fun Fact: Lentils are one of the oldest cultivated crops, with evidence of their consumption dating back to 11,000 years ago.

Chef Insights: Feel free to throw in some vegetables like bell peppers or zucchini to make it a complete meal. The curry will thicken as it sits, so add a bit of water when reheating.

Mains - Vegetarian

STUFFED BELL PEPPERS

INGREDIENTS:

4 BELL PEPPERS, HALVED AND SEEDS REMOVED
1 CUP COOKED RICE
1 CAN BLACK BEANS, DRAINED
1 CUP CORN KERNELS
1 CUP SALSA
1 TEASPOON CUMIN

RECIPE:

1. Mix rice, black beans, corn, salsa, and cumin.
2. Stuff the bell pepper halves with the mixture.
3. Bake at 375°F (190°C) for 30 minutes, or until peppers are tender.

Fun Fact: Bell peppers are fruits, not vegetables, because they contain seeds and come from a flowering plant.

Chef Insight: You can also add some shredded cheese on top if you're not going strictly plant-based. It will add a gooey, melty texture.

SWEET POTATO CURRY

INGREDIENTS:

2 SWEET POTATOES, CUBED
1 CAN CHICKPEAS, DRAINED
1 CAN COCONUT MILK
1 TABLESPOON CURRY PASTE
1 LIME, JUICED

RECIPE:

1. Sauté sweet potatoes until slightly softened.
2. Add curry paste and stir to coat.
3. Add chickpeas and coconut milk, bringing to a simmer.
4. Cook until sweet potatoes are tender, finishing with lime juice.

Fun Fact: Sweet potatoes are a great source of beta-carotene, fiber, and vitamins.

Chef Insight: The natural sweetness of sweet potatoes balances the spice and complexity of curry flavors beautifully.

Mains - Vegetarian

CHICKPEA SALAD

INGREDIENTS:

2 CANS (15 OZ EACH) CHICKPEAS, DRAINED AND RINSED
1 MEDIUM CUCUMBER, DICED
1 RED BELL PEPPER, DICED
1/4 CUP RED ONION, FINELY CHOPPED

1/4 CUP FRESH PARSLEY, CHOPPED
1/4 CUP FRESH MINT, CHOPPED
1 LEMON, JUICED
2 TBSP OLIVE OIL
SALT AND PEPPER TO TASTE

RECIPE:

1. In a large bowl, combine the drained and rinsed chickpeas, diced cucumber, diced red bell pepper, and finely chopped red onion.
2. Add in the chopped parsley and mint.
3. In a separate small bowl, whisk together the lemon juice, olive oil, salt, and pepper.
4. Pour the dressing over the salad ingredients.
5. Toss everything together until well combined.
6. Serve immediately or let it chill in the refrigerator for a few hours to let the flavors meld together.

Fun Fact: Chickpeas, also known as garbanzo beans, are one of the earliest cultivated legumes. They've been grown in Middle Eastern countries for thousands of years!

Chef Insights: If you have time, let the salad sit in the fridge for at least 30 minutes before serving. This allows the flavors to meld together, making the salad even more delicious. You can also add feta cheese or avocado for extra creaminess.

Beyond Instant Noodles. 200 Quick & Easy College Recipes

VEGAN TACOS

INGREDIENTS:

1 CAN BLACK BEANS, DRAINED AND RINSED
1 AVOCADO, DICED
1 CUP LETTUCE, SHREDDED
1/2 CUP VEGAN CHEESE, SHREDDED
1 TOMATO, DICED
CORN TORTILLAS

RECIPE:

1. Heat the black beans in a small pot, seasoning with a pinch of salt.
2. Prepare the corn tortillas by either warming them in a skillet or the oven.
3. Assemble the tacos by layering beans, lettuce, avocado, tomato, and vegan cheese.
4. Serve immediately with your favorite salsa or hot sauce.

Fun Fact: Tacos have been around for hundreds of years, but the pre-filled taco shell is a relatively new invention, appearing in the 20th century.

Chef Insight: Opt for corn tortillas for a more traditional and gluten-free option. They lend a unique texture and flavor to your tacos.

Mains - Vegetarian

MUSHROOM RISOTTO

INGREDIENTS:

1 1/2 CUPS ARBORIO RICE
1 LB MUSHROOMS, SLICED
1 ONION, DICED
4 CUPS VEGETABLE BROTH, HEATED
1/2 CUP WHITE WINE
2 TABLESPOONS OLIVE OIL
1/4 CUP VEGAN PARMESAN, GRATED

RECIPE:

1. In a large pan, sauté the onions and mushrooms in olive oil until softened.
2. Add the rice and cook, stirring, until translucent.
3. Deglaze the pan with white wine and cook until mostly evaporated.
4. Add a ladle of hot vegetable broth, stirring constantly until absorbed. Repeat until rice is creamy and al dente.
5. Finish with vegan Parmesan.

Fun Fact: Risotto is an Italian dish that has been around since the 16th century. The key to a great risotto is the rice; Arborio rice is the most commonly used.

Chef Insight: The key to a perfect risotto is constant stirring. This releases the starches in the rice, leading to that characteristic creamy texture.

Beyond Instant Noodles. 200 Quick & Easy College Recipes

Sides

Sides

GARLIC BREAD

INGREDIENTS:

1 BAGUETTE
1/2 CUP UNSALTED BUTTER, SOFTENED
4 CLOVES GARLIC, MINCED
2 TABLESPOONS PARSLEY, CHOPPED
SALT TO TASTE

RECIPE:

1. Mix softened butter, minced garlic, chopped parsley, and salt.
2. Slice the baguette and spread the garlic butter mixture on each piece.
3. Bake at 375°F (190°C) until golden and crispy.

Fun Fact: Garlic has been used as both food and medicine in many cultures for thousands of years.

Chef Insight: Choose a quality baguette; it makes a difference. The crunch and chew of the bread should complement the garlic butter perfectly.

MASHED POTATOES

INGREDIENTS:

4 LARGE RUSSET POTATOES, PEELED
AND CUBED
1 CUP MILK
4 TBSP UNSALTED BUTTER

SALT AND PEPPER TO TASTE
OPTIONAL: MINCED GARLIC, CHIVES,
OR CREAM CHEESE FOR FLAVOR

RECIPE:

1. Place the cubed potatoes in a large pot and fill it with enough water to cover them. Add a generous pinch of salt.
2. Bring the water to a boil and cook the potatoes until they are fork-tender, around 15-20 minutes.
3. Drain the potatoes and return them to the pot.
4. Heat the milk and butter in a small saucepan until the butter is melted.
5. Pour the milk and butter mixture over the potatoes.
6. Mash the potatoes using a potato masher until smooth. Season with salt and pepper to taste.
7. If desired, mix in minced garlic, chives, or cream cheese for extra flavor.

Fun Fact: Did you know that potatoes were first domesticated in Peru around 8000 to 5000 BC? They've come a long way to become one of the most versatile ingredients in global cuisines.

Chef Insight: Use Russet potatoes for the fluffiest, smoothest, and most flavor-packed mash. Waxy potatoes can turn gummy when mashed. Also, don't skip the step of heating your milk and butter; this helps achieve a creamy texture.

Sides

GRILLED ASPARAGUS

INGREDIENTS:

1 BUNCH OF ASPARAGUS SPEARS, TRIMMED
2 TABLESPOONS OLIVE OIL
1 GARLIC CLOVE, MINCED
ZEST OF 1 LEMON
SALT AND PEPPER TO TASTE
OPTIONAL: PARMESAN CHEESE FOR GARNISH

RECIPE:

1. Preheat your grill to medium-high heat.
2. In a mixing bowl, toss the asparagus spears with olive oil, minced garlic, lemon zest, salt, and pepper.
3. Place the asparagus directly on the grill grates. Grill for 5-7 minutes, turning occasionally, until they're tender and have char marks.
4. Remove the asparagus from the grill and, if desired, sprinkle with Parmesan cheese for garnish before serving.

Fun Fact: Did you know that asparagus can make your urine smell funny? This is due to a compound called asparagusic acid, which breaks down into sulfur-containing compounds during digestion. Not everyone can detect the smell, though, as it's a genetic trait!

Chef Insights: When shopping for asparagus, look for firm, bright green spears with tight tips. Want to add more flavor? A sprinkle of red pepper flakes or a dash of balsamic reduction can take your grilled asparagus to the next level. Grilling times can vary depending on the thickness of your asparagus spears, so keep an eye on them to avoid overcooking.

RICE PILAF

INGREDIENTS:

1 CUP LONG-GRAIN WHITE RICE
2 TABLESPOONS UNSALTED BUTTER
1 SMALL ONION, FINELY CHOPPED
1 GARLIC CLOVE, MINCED

2 CUPS CHICKEN OR VEGETABLE BROTH
SALT AND PEPPER TO TASTE
OPTIONAL: 1/4 CUP CHOPPED FRESH PARSLEY FOR GARNISH

RECIPE:

1. In a large skillet, melt the butter over medium heat. Add the chopped onion and sauté until it's translucent.
2. Add the minced garlic and rice, cooking until the rice is lightly toasted, about 2-3 minutes.
3. Pour in the broth and bring the mixture to a boil. Reduce heat to low, cover, and simmer for 18-20 minutes, or until the rice is tender and the liquid is absorbed.
4. Fluff the rice with a fork, and season with salt and pepper to taste. Garnish with chopped parsley if desired.

Fun Fact: The term "pilaf" is borrowed into English from the Turkish "pilav," which in turn comes from the Persian "polow." Despite its Middle Eastern origins, versions of pilaf can be found in almost every cuisine!

Chef Insights: You can add ingredients like toasted almonds, golden raisins, or sautéed vegetables to customize your pilaf. Always rinse your rice in cold water before cooking to remove excess starch, which can make the rice gummy. Try using a fork to fluff the rice. A spoon may inadvertently mash the grains, making it dense.

Sides

ROASTED BRUSSELS SPROUTS

INGREDIENTS:

1 LB BRUSSELS SPROUTS, TRIMMED AND HALVED
3 TABLESPOONS OLIVE OIL
SALT AND PEPPER TO TASTE
OPTIONAL: 2 CLOVES GARLIC, MINCED
OPTIONAL: 1/4 CUP GRATED PARMESAN CHEESE

RECIPE:

1. Preheat your oven to 400°F (200°C). Line a baking sheet with parchment paper.
2. In a large mixing bowl, toss the Brussels sprouts with olive oil. Make sure they're evenly coated.
3. Spread the Brussels sprouts on the baking sheet in a single layer. Season with salt, pepper, and minced garlic if using.
4. Roast in the oven for 20-25 minutes, stirring halfway through. The sprouts should be golden brown and slightly crispy on the edges.
5. If using, sprinkle the roasted Brussels sprouts with grated Parmesan cheese while they are still hot.

Fun Fact: Did you know Brussels sprouts grow on a stalk? If you ever get the chance to buy them this way, do it! They're incredibly fresh and have a slightly sweeter flavor when bought on the stalk.

Chef Insights: The key to getting crispy Brussels sprouts is to make sure they're dry before you coat them with oil. Any moisture will steam them, making them soggy.

QUINOA SALAD

INGREDIENTS:

1 CUP QUINOA, RINSED
1 CUCUMBER, DICED
1 RED BELL PEPPER, DICED
1/4 CUP FRESH MINT, CHOPPED
LEMON VINAIGRETTE (LEMON JUICE, OLIVE OIL, SALT, AND PEPPER)

RECIPE:

1. Cook quinoa according to package directions.
2. Toss cooked quinoa with cucumber, red bell pepper, and mint.
3. Drizzle with lemon vinaigrette and toss to combine.

Fun Fact: Quinoa is not a grain; it's a seed from a plant related to spinach, chard, and beets.

Chef Insight: Always rinse quinoa before cooking to remove its natural coating, called saponin, which can make it taste bitter or soapy.

Sides

MAC AND CHEESE

INGREDIENTS:

3 TBSP. UNSALTED BUTTER
2 CUPS WHOLE MILK
1 ½ TSP SALT
3/4 TSP GARLIC POWDER
3/4 TSP FRESHLY GROUND COARSE BLACK PEPPER
1/3 CUPS FLOUR
5 OZ SMOKED CHEDDAR, SHREDDED
1 OZ COLBY JACK, SHREDDED
3/4 LB CAVATAPPI PASTA

RECIPE:

1. Melt butter over medium-low in a medium-sized saucepan.
2. In a large saucepan or Dutch oven, stir together the milk, garlic powder, salt, pepper. Heat over medium heat.
3. Add flour to melted butter and stir together (should look like wet sand) to make a roux.
4. Add roux to hot milk and stir together well.
5. Stir in cheeses and mix until melted and well incorporated.
6. Stir in cooked cavatappi and serve hot.

Fun Fact: The first modern recipe for mac and cheese was featured in the famous cookbook, "The Virginia Housewife," published in 1824.

Chef Insight: For an extra touch of sophistication, top the mac and cheese with breadcrumbs and bake until golden brown.

Beyond Instant Noodles. 200 Quick & Easy College Recipes

CREAMED SPINACH

INGREDIENTS:

1 LB FRESH SPINACH
1/2 CUP HEAVY CREAM
2 CLOVES GARLIC, MINCED
SALT AND NUTMEG TO TASTE

RECIPE:

1. Sauté garlic until fragrant.
2. Add spinach and cook until wilted.
3. Stir in heavy cream, salt, and a pinch of nutmeg. Cook until thickened.

Fun Fact: Spinach is originally from Persia (modern Iran). It made its way to Europe in the 12th century.

Chef Insight: Using freshly grated nutmeg can elevate this simple dish to new heights.

Sides

SEASONED ROASTED SWEET POTATOES

INGREDIENTS:

3 LARGE SWEET POTATOES, PEELED AND CUT INTO LONG WEDGES
2 TBSP OLIVE OIL
3/4 TSP SALT
1/4 TSP FRESHLY GROUND BLACK PEPPER
1/2 TSP CHILI POWDER
1/2 TSP SMOKED PAPRIKA
1/2 TSP CUMIN
1/2 TSP GARLIC POWDER

RECIPE:

1. Preheat oven to 425°F (218°C).
2. Place sweet potatoes in a large bowl and drizzle with olive oil; toss to coat potatoes well.
3. Combine all spices in a small bowl, then sprinkle over potatoes covering all sides.
4. Spread out potatoes in an even layer on a sheet pan.
5. Bake for 30 minutes, flipping once after 15 minutes.

Fun Fact: North Carolina produced 1.8 billion pounds of sweet potatoes in 2021, accounting for roughly 64% of all production in the U.S.

Chef Insight: Using a good-quality, heavy-duty baking sheet can improve the evenness of roasting. Cheap, thin pans are more likely to cause uneven cooking.

GREEK TZATZIKI

INGREDIENTS:

2 CUPS GREEK YOGURT
1 CUCUMBER, PEELED AND GRATED
2-3 CLOVES GARLIC, MINCED
JUICE OF 1 LEMON

2 TABLESPOONS FRESH DILL, FINELY
CHOPPED
2 TABLESPOONS EXTRA-VIRGIN
OLIVE OIL
SALT AND PEPPER TO TASTE

RECIPE:

1. Start by placing the grated cucumber in a sieve over a bowl. Sprinkle with a little salt and let it sit for 10-15 minutes to drain excess water.
2. In a mixing bowl, combine Greek yogurt, minced garlic, lemon juice, and olive oil.
3. Squeeze the grated cucumber to remove any remaining moisture and then add it to the yogurt mixture.
4. Stir in fresh dill and mix thoroughly.
5. Season with salt and pepper to taste.
6. Chill the tzatziki sauce in the refrigerator for at least an hour before serving to allow flavors to meld together.

Fun Fact: The word "tzatziki" is derived from the Turkish word "cacık," which itself was borrowed from the Armenian word "cacıg."

Chef Insights: It's crucial to drain the cucumber well to avoid a watery tzatziki. The sauce becomes more flavorful as it sits, so making it in advance is a good idea. Tzatziki can be used in a variety of ways — as a dip for veggies, as a sauce in gyros, or even as a dressing for a Mediterranean-style salad.

Breads

Beyond Instant Noodles. 200 Quick & Easy College Recipes

SOURDOUGH BREAD

INGREDIENTS:

1 CUP SOURDOUGH STARTER
1 1/2 CUPS WARM WATER
4 CUPS BREAD FLOUR
2 TEASPOONS SALT

RECIPE:

1. Mix starter, warm water, and 3 cups of flour. Let it rest for 30 minutes.
2. Add salt and remaining flour, knead until smooth.
3. Let rise for 4-8 hours, then shape into a loaf.
4. Bake at 450°F (230°C) for 30-40 minutes.

Fun Fact: The oldest recorded sourdough bread was made by the ancient Egyptians around 1500 BC.

Chef Insight: Your sourdough starter is like a pet; feed it regularly for the best results.

Breads

FOCACCIA

INGREDIENTS:

1 1/2 CUPS WARM WATER (110°F)
2 TSP SUGAR
2 1/4 TSP ACTIVE DRY YEAST
4 CUPS ALL-PURPOSE FLOUR
1/4 CUP EXTRA-VIRGIN OLIVE OIL,

PLUS MORE FOR GREASING AND
DRIZZLING
1 TSP SALT
COARSE SEA SALT, FOR SPRINKLING
FRESH ROSEMARY SPRIGS, FOR
GARNISH

RECIPE:

1. In a small bowl, combine warm water and sugar. Sprinkle yeast on top and let it sit for about 5 minutes until frothy.
2. In a large bowl, combine flour, 1/4 cup olive oil, and 1 teaspoon salt. Add the yeast mixture and mix until a dough forms.
3. Knead the dough on a lightly floured surface until smooth and elastic, about 10 minutes.
4. Place the dough in a greased bowl, cover with a damp cloth, and let rise in a warm area for 1-2 hours, or until doubled in size.
5. Preheat the oven to 400°F (200°C). Punch down the dough and transfer it to a greased baking sheet. Using your fingers, poke holes all over the dough. Drizzle it with olive oil.
6. Sprinkle the dough with coarse sea salt and fresh rosemary.
7. Bake for 20-25 minutes, until golden brown. Drizzle with more olive oil before serving, if desired.

Fun Fact: Focaccia dates back to ancient times.

Chef Insights: For an authentic touch, add sliced olives or sundried tomatoes to the dough before baking. The dough's nooks and crannies absorb the olive oil, resulting in a more flavorful bread.

BAGUETTE

INGREDIENTS:

4 CUPS BREAD FLOUR
1 1/2 CUPS WARM WATER
2 1/4 TEASPOONS INSTANT YEAST
2 TEASPOONS SALT

RECIPE:

1. Combine all ingredients and knead until smooth.
2. Divide into 2-3 long loaves and let rise for 1 hour.
3. Bake at 450°F (230°C) for 25-30 minutes.

Fun Fact: The baguette became popular in France during the 1920s but is considered to have roots that go much further back.

Chef Insight: For that quintessential crispy crust, create steam in the oven by placing a pan of hot water on the bottom rack.

Breads

CIABATTA

INGREDIENTS:

4 CUPS BREAD FLOUR
1 1/2 CUPS WARM WATER
2 TEASPOONS SALT
1 1/2 TEASPOONS INSTANT YEAST

RECIPE:

1. Combine water and yeast. Add flour and salt, mixing until shaggy.
2. Knead for 8-10 minutes until smooth.
3. Let it rise for 1-2 hours.
4. Shape into a rectangular loaf and bake at 425°F (220°C) for 25-30 minutes.

Fun Fact: "Ciabatta" means "slipper" in Italian, named for the bread's slipper-like shape.

Chef Insight: This bread is perfect for paninis due to its sturdy yet airy texture.

CORNBREAD

INGREDIENTS:

1 CUP CORNMEAL
1 CUP ALL-PURPOSE FLOUR
4 TEASPOONS BAKING POWDER
1/4 CUP SUGAR
1 CUP MILK
1/4 CUP MELTED BUTTER
2 EGGS

RECIPE:

1. Mix dry ingredients together.
2. Add milk, butter, and eggs, stirring just until moist.
3. Pour into a greased pan and bake at 425°F (220°C) for 20-25 minutes.

Fun Fact: Cornbread is native to the Americas and was a staple in Native American diets long before European settlers arrived.

Chef Insight: To add some zing, consider adding jalapeños or cheddar cheese to the batter.

BANANA BREAD

INGREDIENTS:

1 3/4 CUPS ALL-PURPOSE FLOUR
2/3 CUP SUGAR
1 TSP BAKING POWDER
1/2 TSP SALT
1/4 TSP BAKING SODA
1 STICK BUTTER, SOFTENED
1 CUP RIPE BANANAS (3), MASHED
2 EGGS, BEATEN

RECIPE:

1. Preheat oven to 350°F (180°C). Grease a 9x5-inch loaf pan.
2. In a large bowl, mix the first 5 ingredients. Using a fork or your fingers, rub butter into mixture until it resembles coarse crumbs.
3. Mix together bananas and eggs, and stir into dry ingredients just until flour is moistened. Spoon batter evenly into loaf pan.
4. Bake for 55 minutes or until a toothpick comes out clean. Cool on wire rack for 10 minutes; remove from pan and finish cooling on wire rack.

Fun Fact: The first cookbooks featuring recipes for banana bread were published during the Great Depression.

Chef Insight: Overripe bananas are your best friend for a moist and flavorful banana bread.

PUMPKIN BREAD

INGREDIENTS:

1 3/4 CUPS ALL-PURPOSE FLOUR
1 TEASPOON BAKING SODA
1/2 TEASPOON SALT
1/2 TEASPOON CINNAMON
1/2 TEASPOON NUTMEG
1/2 CUP SUGAR
1/2 CUP BROWN SUGAR
1/2 CUP VEGETABLE OIL
2 EGGS
1 CUP CANNED PUMPKIN
1/4 CUP WATER
1/2 TEASPOON VANILLA EXTRACT

RECIPE:

1. Combine dry ingredients in one bowl and wet ingredients in another.
2. Add wet to dry, mix until just combined.
3. Bake in a loaf pan at 350°F (175°C) for 60-70 minutes.

Fun Fact: Pumpkin bread gained popularity in the U.S. in the early 18th century.

Chef Insight: Add a crumb topping or chocolate chips to kick it up a notch.

Breads

BRIOCHE

INGREDIENTS:

4 CUPS BREAD FLOUR
1/4 CUP SUGAR
2 1/4 TEASPOONS INSTANT YEAST
1/2 TEASPOON SALT
1/2 CUP WARM MILK
3 EGGS
1 CUP UNSALTED BUTTER, SOFTENED

RECIPE:

1. Combine flour, sugar, yeast, and salt.
2. Add milk and eggs, knead until smooth.
3. Gradually add butter while kneading.
4. Let rise for 2-3 hours, then shape into a loaf.
5. Bake at 375°F (190°C) for 30-35 minutes.

Fun Fact: Brioche originated from France and is often considered a hybrid between bread and pastry due to its high butter content.

Chef Insight: Always use high-quality butter for a truly rich brioche.

CHALLAH

INGREDIENTS:

4 CUPS BREAD FLOUR
1/2 CUP SUGAR
2 TEASPOONS SALT
2 1/4 TEASPOONS INSTANT YEAST
1 CUP WARM WATER
2 EGGS + 1 FOR EGG WASH
1/2 CUP VEGETABLE OIL

RECIPE:

1. Combine flour, sugar, salt, and yeast.
2. Add water, 2 eggs, and oil. Knead until smooth.
3. Let rise for 1-2 hours, then braid into a loaf.
4. Brush with egg wash and bake at 375°F (190°C) for 30-35 minutes.

Fun Fact: Challah is a special bread in Jewish cuisine, usually braided and typically eaten on ceremonial occasions such as Shabbat.

Chef Insight: The art of braiding the dough isn't just for show; it represents unity and love.

Breads

PITA BREAD

INGREDIENTS:

1 CUP WARM WATER (110°F)
1 TABLESPOON SUGAR
2 1/4 TEASPOONS ACTIVE DRY YEAST

3 CUPS ALL-PURPOSE FLOUR
1 TEASPOON SALT
2 TABLESPOONS OLIVE OIL

RECIPE:

1. Mix warm water and sugar in a small bowl. Add yeast and let it sit for about 5 minutes, until frothy.
2. In a large bowl, combine flour and salt. Make a well in the center and pour in the yeast mixture and olive oil.
3. Mix the ingredients to form a dough. Knead for about 10 minutes until the dough becomes smooth and elastic.
4. Place the dough in a lightly oiled bowl, cover it with a damp cloth, and let it rise for 1-2 hours, or until it doubles in size.
5. Preheat your oven to 475°F (245°C). If you have a pizza stone, place it in the oven to heat.
6. Divide the dough into 8 equal portions and roll each into a ball. Roll out each ball into a circle, about 1/4-inch thick.
7. Place the rolled-out dough onto the preheated pizza stone or a baking sheet. Bake for 2-3 minutes on each side, or until the bread puffs up and takes on a slight golden color.

Fun Fact: Pita bread is one of the oldest known breads and is believed to have originated over 4,000 years ago.

Chef Insights: Pita bread is all about the puff. If it doesn't puff up in the oven, it won't have that classic pocket. A very hot oven helps achieve this.

Beyond Instant Noodles. 200 Quick & Easy College Recipes

Pasta

Pasta

PENNE ARRABBIATA

INGREDIENTS:

400G PENNE PASTA
2 CUPS TOMATO SAUCE
3 GARLIC CLOVES, MINCED
1 TEASPOON RED PEPPER FLAKES
OLIVE OIL
SALT TO TASTE
FRESH BASIL LEAVES FOR GARNISH

RECIPE:

1. Cook Penne according to package instructions until al dente.
2. In a saucepan, heat olive oil and sauté garlic until fragrant.
3. Add red pepper flakes and tomato sauce. Simmer for 10-15 minutes.
4. Toss the cooked Penne into the sauce.
5. Garnish with fresh basil leaves before serving.

Fun Fact: "Arrabbiata" means "angry" in Italian, which refers to the spiciness of the chili peppers in the sauce.

Chef Insight: For an authentic touch, use San Marzano tomatoes for your sauce. They are less acidic and sweeter than regular tomatoes.

Beyond Instant Noodles. 200 Quick & Easy College Recipes

FETTUCCINE ALFREDO

INGREDIENTS:

400G FETTUCCINE PASTA
1 CUP HEAVY CREAM
1/2 CUP UNSALTED BUTTER
1 CUP GRATED PARMESAN CHEESE
SALT AND BLACK PEPPER TO TASTE

RECIPE:

1. Cook Fettuccine according to package instructions until al dente.
2. In a saucepan, melt butter into the heavy cream on low heat.
3. Add the grated Parmesan cheese and stir until melted.
4. Toss the cooked Fettuccine into the sauce.
5. Season with salt and pepper to taste.

Fun Fact: Despite its fame in America, Fettuccine Alfredo is actually not that popular in Italy.

Chef Insight: The secret to a great Alfredo sauce is the quality of Parmesan used. Invest in a high-quality, aged Parmesan for a richer taste.

Pasta

PESTO LINGUINE

INGREDIENTS:

400G LINGUINE PASTA
2 CUPS FRESH BASIL LEAVES
1/2 CUP PINE NUTS
1/2 CUP GRATED PARMESAN CHEESE
2 GARLIC CLOVES
1/2 CUP OLIVE OIL
SALT AND PEPPER TO TASTE

RECIPE:

1. Cook Linguine according to package instructions until al dente.
2. In a food processor, blend basil, pine nuts, Parmesan, and garlic.
3. Slowly add olive oil while blending. Season with salt and pepper.
4. Toss the cooked Linguine with the pesto sauce.

Fun Fact: Pesto originated from Genoa, Italy, and the term "pesto" comes from the Italian word "pestare," which means to crush.

Chef Insight: Toast the pine nuts lightly before blending for a richer flavor. Also, you can experiment with different nuts like almonds or walnuts for a unique twist.

SPAGHETTI BOLOGNESE

INGREDIENTS:

400G SPAGHETTI PASTA
500G GROUND BEEF
1 ONION, FINELY CHOPPED
2 GARLIC CLOVES, MINCED
2 CUPS TOMATO SAUCE
1/2 CUP RED WINE (OPTIONAL)
OLIVE OIL
SALT AND PEPPER TO TASTE

RECIPE:

1. Cook Spaghetti according to package instructions until al dente.
2. In a skillet, heat olive oil and sauté onions and garlic.
3. Add ground beef and cook until browned.
4. Add tomato sauce and red wine. Simmer for 30-45 minutes.
5. Toss the cooked Spaghetti with the sauce.

Fun Fact: Bolognese sauce originates from Bologna, Italy, and the Italian version, called "Ragù alla Bolognese," is often served with tagliatelle rather than spaghetti.

Chef Insight: Adding a splash of red wine deepens the flavors, but make sure to cook it down thoroughly to eliminate the alcohol content.

Pasta

LASAGNA

INGREDIENTS:

9 LASAGNA NOODLES
1 LB GROUND BEEF
1 LB RICOTTA CHEESE
1 CUP GRATED PARMESAN CHEESE
3 CUPS SHREDDED MOZZARELLA CHEESE
2 CUPS TOMATO SAUCE
1 ONION, CHOPPED
2 GARLIC CLOVES, MINCED
OLIVE OIL
SALT AND PEPPER TO TASTE

RECIPE:

1. Preheat oven to 375°F (190°C).
2. Cook lasagna noodles according to package instructions.
3. In a skillet, heat olive oil and sauté onions and garlic.
4. Add ground beef and cook until browned. Stir in tomato sauce and simmer.
5. In a baking dish, layer noodles, ricotta, mozzarella, Parmesan, and meat sauce.
6. Repeat layers and finish with a layer of cheese on top.
7. Bake for 25-30 minutes or until bubbly and golden.

Fun Fact: Lasagna is believed to have originated in Ancient Greece, where they had a dish called "Laganon," made from layers of pasta and sauce.

Chef Insight: For a richer lasagna, consider adding a layer of béchamel sauce in between the noodles and meat.

TORTELLINI SOUP

INGREDIENTS:

1 LB CHEESE TORTELLINI
4 CUPS CHICKEN BROTH
1 CUP SPINACH LEAVES, CHOPPED
1 ONION, CHOPPED
2 GARLIC CLOVES, MINCED
2 TABLESPOONS OLIVE OIL
SALT AND PEPPER TO TASTE

RECIPE:

1. In a large pot, heat olive oil and sauté onions and garlic.
2. Add chicken broth and bring to a boil.
3. Add tortellini and cook until they float to the top.
4. Stir in spinach and cook until wilted.
5. Season with salt and pepper to taste.

Fun Fact: Tortellini is often referred to as "belly button" pasta due to its navel-like shape.

Chef Insight: Fresh tortellini is preferable for this soup, but frozen works well too. Just adjust the cooking time accordingly.

Pasta

AGLIO E OLIO

INGREDIENTS:

400G SPAGHETTI
4-5 GARLIC CLOVES, THINLY SLICED
1/4 TEASPOON RED PEPPER FLAKES
1/2 CUP EXTRA-VIRGIN OLIVE OIL
PARSLEY, CHOPPED FOR GARNISH
SALT TO TASTE

RECIPE:

1. Cook spaghetti according to package instructions until al dente.
2. In a skillet, heat olive oil over low heat. Add garlic and red pepper flakes.
3. Cook until garlic turns golden but not brown.
4. Toss the cooked spaghetti in the garlic oil.
5. Garnish with chopped parsley.

Fun Fact: Aglio e Olio literally means "garlic and oil" in Italian. It's a traditional Italian pasta dish coming from Naples.

Chef Insight: The key to a great Aglio e Olio is to infuse the oil without burning the garlic. Keep the heat low and your eyes on the pan.

PASTA PRIMAVERA

INGREDIENTS:

400G PENNE PASTA
1 CUP CHERRY TOMATOES, HALVED
1 BELL PEPPER, SLICED
1 ZUCCHINI, SLICED
1 CUP ASPARAGUS, CHOPPED
2 GARLIC CLOVES, MINCED
OLIVE OIL
SALT AND PEPPER TO TASTE

RECIPE:

1. Cook penne according to package instructions until al dente.
2. In a large skillet, heat olive oil and sauté garlic until fragrant.
3. Add the vegetables and sauté until tender but still crisp.
4. Toss the cooked penne with the sautéed vegetables.
5. Season with salt and pepper to taste.

Fun Fact: "Primavera" means spring in Italian, and this dish celebrates the fresh produce available during the season.

Chef Insight: Feel free to vary the veggies based on what's seasonal. The fresher the produce, the better your Primavera will taste.

Pasta

LOBSTER RAVIOLI

INGREDIENTS:

1 LB LOBSTER MEAT, COOKED AND CHOPPED
1 CUP RICOTTA CHEESE
1/4 CUP GRATED PARMESAN CHEESE
1 EGG, BEATEN
2 CUPS PASTA DOUGH (HOMEMADE OR STORE-BOUGHT)
2 CUPS MARINARA SAUCE
SALT AND PEPPER TO TASTE

RECIPE:

1. In a bowl, mix lobster meat, ricotta, Parmesan, and beaten egg. Season with salt and pepper.
2. Roll out the pasta dough and cut it into squares.
3. Place a spoonful of lobster filling in the center of each square.
4. Fold the dough over the filling to form a triangle or half-moon shape. Seal the edges.
5. Cook the ravioli in boiling salted water for 4-5 minutes or until they float to the top.
6. Serve with warm marinara sauce.

Fun Fact: Ravioli dates back to 14th-century Italy and was initially a way to use up leftover meat.

Chef Insight: Fresh pasta is the key to great ravioli. If you're short on time, some Italian delis sell fresh pasta sheets that can be used.

GNOCCHI

INGREDIENTS:

2 CUPS POTATO, COOKED AND MASHED
1 1/2 CUPS ALL-PURPOSE FLOUR
1 EGG, BEATEN
SALT TO TASTE

RECIPE:

1. In a large bowl, mix mashed potato, flour, and beaten egg.
2. Knead until the dough forms. Add salt to taste.
3. Divide the dough into ropes and cut into 1-inch pieces.
4. Roll each piece on a fork to create ridges.
5. Boil in salted water until the gnocchi float to the surface. Drain.
6. Serve with your choice of sauce.

Fun Fact: Gnocchi means "lumps" in Italian, and these soft dough dumplings can be made from various ingredients, including semolina, cheese, and even breadcrumbs.

Chef Insight: The secret to fluffy gnocchi is using the right potato variety. Russet potatoes work well because they're starchy and not too watery.

Desserts

CHOCOLATE CAKE

INGREDIENTS:

1 3/4 CUPS ALL-PURPOSE FLOUR
1 1/2 TEASPOONS BAKING POWDER
1 1/2 TEASPOONS BAKING SODA
3/4 CUP UNSWEETENED COCOA POWDER
2 CUPS SUGAR
2 EGGS
1 CUP WHOLE MILK
1/2 CUP VEGETABLE OIL
2 TEASPOONS VANILLA EXTRACT
1 CUP BOILING WATER

RECIPE:

1. Preheat oven to 350°F (175°C). Grease and flour two 9-inch round cake pans.
2. In a large bowl, sift together flour, cocoa powder, baking powder, and baking soda.
3. Add sugar, eggs, milk, oil, and vanilla. Mix very well.
4. Stir in boiling water until smooth.
5. Pour the batter into prepared pans and bake for 30-35 minutes.

Fun Fact: The history of chocolate cake goes back to ancient times, but it was only in the 18th century that chocolate was incorporated into cake batter.

Chef Insight: Always sift your cocoa powder and flour for a lighter and fluffier cake.

Desserts

APPLE PIE

INGREDIENTS:

2 PIE CRUSTS (STORE-BOUGHT OR HOMEMADE)
6 CUPS SLICED AND PEELED APPLES
3/4 CUP SUGAR
1 TEASPOON CINNAMON
1/2 TEASPOON NUTMEG
1 TABLESPOON LEMON JUICE
2 TABLESPOONS BUTTER, CUBED

RECIPE:

1. Preheat oven to 425°F (220°C).
2. Mix sliced apples with sugar, cinnamon, nutmeg, and lemon juice.
3. Roll out one pie crust and place it in a 9-inch pie dish.
4. Fill with apple mixture and dot with butter.
5. Place the second crust on top and seal the edges. Make slits for steam to escape.
6. Bake for 45-50 minutes or until golden brown.

Fun Fact: The first apple pie recipe dates back to England in 1381. The original recipe included figs, raisins, and pears as well as apples.

Chef Insight: Use a mix of tart and sweet apples for a well-balanced pie filling.

CHEESECAKE

INGREDIENTS:

1 1/2 CUPS GRAHAM CRACKER CRUMBS
1/4 CUP SUGAR
1/2 CUP MELTED BUTTER
16 OZ CREAM CHEESE, SOFTENED
1 CUP SUGAR
4 EGGS
1 TEASPOON VANILLA EXTRACT
1 CUP SOUR CREAM

RECIPE:

1. Preheat the oven to 325°F (160°C).
2. Combine graham cracker crumbs, 1/4 cup sugar, and melted butter. Press into the bottom of a 9-inch springform pan.
3. Beat cream cheese until smooth. Add 1 cup sugar, eggs, and vanilla extract. Mix until well combined.
4. Pour the cream cheese mixture over the crust.
5. Bake for 55-60 minutes or until the center is set.
6. Allow to cool and then top with sour cream.

Fun Fact: Cheesecake has been delighting taste buds for thousands of years; it dates back to ancient Greece and was even served to athletes at the first Olympic games!

Chef Insight: To avoid cracks in your cheesecake, don't overmix the batter, and consider using a water bath during baking.

Desserts

PANNA COTTA

INGREDIENTS:

2 CUPS HEAVY CREAM
1/2 CUP SUGAR
1 TEASPOON VANILLA EXTRACT
2 1/4 TEASPOONS GELATIN
3 TABLESPOONS COLD WATER

RECIPE:

1. In a small bowl, sprinkle gelatin over cold water and let it sit for a few minutes.
2. Heat the cream and sugar in a pan until hot but not boiling. Remove from heat.
3. Add the soaked gelatin and vanilla extract to the hot cream. Stir until completely dissolved.
4. Pour into individual molds or cups.
5. Chill in the fridge for at least 4 hours, until set.

Fun Fact: Panna Cotta means "cooked cream" in Italian. It's a simple yet elegant dessert that originated in the Piedmont region of Italy.

Chef Insight: The perfect panna cotta should have a slight "wobble" but hold its shape when unmolded. Using the right amount of gelatin is key.

Beyond Instant Noodles. 200 Quick & Easy College Recipes

CHOCOLATE CHIP COOKIES

INGREDIENTS:

1 CUP (2 STICKS) UNSALTED BUTTER, SOFTENED
3/4 CUP GRANULATED SUGAR
3/4 CUP BROWN SUGAR, PACKED
2 LARGE EGGS
1 TEASPOON VANILLA EXTRACT
3 CUPS ALL-PURPOSE FLOUR
1/2 TEASPOON SALT
1 TEASPOON BAKING SODA
2 CUPS CHOCOLATE CHIPS

RECIPE:

1. Preheat oven to 375°F (190°C). Line a baking sheet with parchment paper.
2. Cream together butter, gr. sugar, and brown sugar until fluffy.
3. Add eggs and vanilla extract; mix well.
4. Combine flour, salt, and baking soda in a separate bowl. Gradually add to wet mixture.
5. Stir in chocolate chips.
6. Drop spoonfuls onto prepared baking sheet and bake for 9-11 minutes.

Fun Fact: The chocolate chip cookie was invented by accident in 1938 by Ruth Wakefield, who ran the Toll House Inn in Whitman, Massachusetts.

Chef Insight: For chewier cookies, chill the dough for at least 30 minutes before baking. This allows the fats to re-solidify, resulting in a chewier texture. Also, invest in good chocolate!

Desserts

BROWNIES

INGREDIENTS:

1/2 CUP (1 STICK) UNSALTED BUTTER, MELTED
1 CUP GRANULATED SUGAR
2 LARGE EGGS
1 TEASPOON VANILLA EXTRACT
1/3 CUP UNSWEETENED COCOA POWDER
1/2 CUP ALL-PURPOSE FLOUR
1/4 TEASPOON SALT
1/4 TEASPOON BAKING POWDER

RECIPE:

1. Preheat oven to 350°F (175°C). Grease a 9x9-inch baking pan.
2. In a large bowl, mix melted butter, sugar, eggs, and vanilla extract.
3. In another bowl, combine cocoa powder, flour, salt, and baking powder.
4. Mix dry ingredients into the wet mixture until combined.
5. Spread into the prepared pan and bake for 20-25 minutes.

Fun Fact: Brownies originated in the U.S. at the end of the 19th century. The first known recipe appeared in the 1897 Sears Roebuck Catalog.

Chef Insight: To test for doneness, insert a toothpick into the center; it should come out with a few moist crumbs.

TIRAMISU

INGREDIENTS:

1 CUP ESPRESSO OR STRONG COFFEE, COOLED
2 TABLESPOONS COFFEE LIQUEUR (OPTIONAL)
3 EGG YOLKS
1/2 CUP SUGAR
8 OZ MASCARPONE CHEESE
1 CUP HEAVY CREAM
1 PACKAGE LADYFINGERS
UNSWEETENED COCOA POWDER, FOR DUSTING

RECIPE:

1. Combine cooled coffee with coffee liqueur, if using. Set aside.
2. Beat egg yolks and sugar until well combined.
3. In a separate bowl, beat mascarpone and cream until thick.
4. Fold the egg yolk mixture into the mascarpone mixture.
5. Quickly dip ladyfingers into the coffee mixture and layer them in a serving dish.
6. Spread half the mascarpone mixture over the ladyfingers.
7. Add another layer of dipped ladyfingers and top with remaining mascarpone mixture.
8. Chill for at least 4 hours. Finish by dusting with cocoa powder.

Fun Fact: Despite its rich history, tiramisu is a relatively modern creation from the 1960s in Italy. The name means "pick me up" in Italian, referring to the energizing ingredients like coffee and sugar.

Chef Insight: Use the best quality coffee you can find for this recipe; it makes a world of difference in the flavor.

Desserts

SANTIAGO CAKE

INGREDIENTS:

1 1/2 CUPS GROUND ALMONDS
1 1/4 CUPS SUGAR
4 LARGE EGGS
ZEST OF 1 LEMON
1/4 TEASPOON GROUND CINNAMON
POWDERED SUGAR, FOR DUSTING

RECIPE:

1. Preheat oven to 350°F (175°C). Grease an 8-inch cake pan and line with parchment paper.
2. In a bowl, mix together ground almonds, sugar, lemon zest, and cinnamon.
3. In another bowl, beat the eggs until frothy.
4. Fold the egg mixture into the almond mixture.
5. Pour the batter into the prepared cake pan.
6. Bake for 40-45 minutes, or until a toothpick inserted into the center comes out clean.
7. Once cooled, dust with powdered sugar.

Fun Fact: Santiago Cake is a traditional Spanish almond cake originating from Galicia. It's often decorated with powdered sugar and the cross of Saint James.

Chef Insight: This is a gluten-free cake, but its texture is moist and rich, thanks to the ground almonds. Almonds also offer a nice alternative to traditional flour-based cakes.

S'MORES

INGREDIENTS:

12 GRAHAM CRACKERS
6 LARGE MARSHMALLOWS
1 LARGE CHOCOLATE BAR, BROKEN INTO SMALLER PIECES

RECIPE:

1. Preheat your oven broiler, or prepare a campfire.
2. Place half of the Graham crackers on a baking sheet.
3. Put a piece of chocolate on each Graham cracker.
4. Top each chocolate piece with a marshmallow.
5. Broil in the oven or cook over a campfire until the marshmallows are golden brown.
6. Place the remaining Graham crackers on top of the marshmallows, pressing down slightly.

Fun Fact: S'mores are a classic American treat, and the name is a contraction of "some more," because you'll always want more!

Chef Insight: For a gourmet twist, try using flavored marshmallows or different types of chocolate, such as dark or white chocolate. The better the chocolate, the better the experience.

Desserts

RICE PUDDING

INGREDIENTS:

1 CUP ARBORIO RICE
4 CUPS WHOLE MILK
1/2 CUP SUGAR
1 TEASPOON VANILLA EXTRACT
1/2 TEASPOON GROUND CINNAMON
ZEST OF 1 LEMON (OPTIONAL)

RECIPE:

1. In a saucepan, combine the rice and 2 cups of milk.
2. Cook over low heat until the milk is mostly absorbed, stirring frequently.
3. Add the remaining milk, sugar, and vanilla extract.
4. Continue cooking, stirring often, until the rice is tender.
5. Remove from heat and stir in the cinnamon and lemon zest, if using.
6. Allow it to cool before serving, or serve warm if you prefer.

Fun Fact: Rice pudding is enjoyed worldwide, with variations existing in many different cultures. The dish dates back to ancient times.

Chef Insight: Arborio rice, typically used for risotto, also works great for rice pudding due to its high starch content, yielding a creamy texture.

Beverages

Beverages

MARGARITA

INGREDIENTS:

2 OZ TEQUILA
1 OZ LIME JUICE
1 OZ TRIPLE SEC
ICE
LIME WEDGE AND SALT FOR GARNISH

RECIPE:

1. Rim the edge of a glass with a lime wedge and dip it into salt.
2. In a shaker, combine tequila, lime juice, and triple sec with ice.
3. Shake well and strain into the glass.
4. Garnish with a lime wedge.

Fun Fact: The Margarita is a classic Mexican cocktail that's been popular since around the 1940s. The true origin is disputed, but it's often enjoyed on Cinco de Mayo.

Chef Insight: Use high-quality tequila for the best flavor. Tequila made from 100% agave is the way to go.

LEMONADE

INGREDIENTS:

1 CUP FRESHLY SQUEEZED LEMON JUICE
1 CUP GRANULATED SUGAR
6 CUPS COLD WATER
LEMON SLICES FOR GARNISH

RECIPE:

1. In a saucepan, heat 1 cup of water and sugar until the sugar is dissolved.
2. In a pitcher, combine the lemon juice, sugar water, and remaining 5 cups of cold water.
3. Stir well and chill before serving.
4. Garnish with lemon slices.

Fun Fact: Lemonade dates back to ancient Egypt and was a staple for Pharaohs and their courts.

Chef Insight: For an aromatic twist, add a sprig of fresh mint or a splash of lavender syrup.

Beverages

SMOOTHIES

INGREDIENTS:

1 BANANA, PEELED
1 CUP FROZEN BERRIES
1/2 CUP GREEK YOGURT
1 CUP ALMOND MILK OR JUICE
1 TABLESPOON HONEY OR MAPLE SYRUP (OPTIONAL)

RECIPE:

1. In a blender, combine all the ingredients.
2. Blend until smooth and creamy.
3. Pour into glasses and serve immediately.

Fun Fact: Smoothies gained widespread popularity in the U.S. during the health food movement of the '60s and '70s.

Chef Insight: Frozen fruits not only make your smoothie cold but also give it a thicker, creamier texture.

KALIMOTXO

INGREDIENTS:

1 PART RED WINE (A YOUNG, FRUITY ONE WORKS BEST)
1 PART COLA
ICE CUBES
1 LIME OR LEMON WEDGE FOR GARNISH

RECIPE:

1. Fill a glass halfway with ice cubes.
2. Add equal parts of red wine and cola to the glass.
3. Stir gently to combine.
4. Garnish with a lime or lemon wedge.

Fun Fact: The Kalimotxo is incredibly popular in the Basque Country and during the Running of the Bulls festival in Pamplona.

Chef Insight: Though this cocktail is straightforward, the choice of wine can make a big difference. Use a wine you'd enjoy on its own, but don't go too expensive—after all, you're mixing it with cola!

Beverages

MILKSHAKE

INGREDIENTS:

2 CUPS VANILLA ICE CREAM
1 CUP WHOLE MILK
1 TEASPOON VANILLA EXTRACT
OPTIONAL: CHOCOLATE SYRUP, WHIPPED CREAM, CHERRY FOR GARNISH

RECIPE:

1. Combine ice cream, milk, and vanilla extract in a blender.
2. Blend until smooth and creamy.
3. Pour into a chilled glass.
4. Optional: Add chocolate syrup, whipped cream, and a cherry on top for garnish.

Fun Fact: The term "milkshake" originally referred to an alcoholic beverage, similar to eggnog. It evolved into the sweet treat we know today in the early 1900s.

Chef Insight: The type of ice cream you choose can drastically change the flavor profile. For a richer shake, opt for premium ice cream.

MIMOSA

INGREDIENTS:

1 PART CHILLED CHAMPAGNE OR SPARKLING WINE
1 PART CHILLED CITRUS JUICE (USUALLY ORANGE JUICE)
ORANGE SLICE FOR GARNISH

RECIPE:

1. Fill half of a champagne flute with chilled citrus juice.
2. Top off with Champagne or sparkling wine.
3. Gently stir to mix.
4. Garnish with an orange slice.

Fun Fact: The Mimosa is named after the yellow mimosa flowers, which are similar in color to the drink.

Chef Insight: Use freshly squeezed orange juice for a brighter, fresher flavor. For a twist, try using grapefruit juice or even a splash of cranberry.

Beverages

HOT CHOCOLATE

INGREDIENTS:

2 CUPS WHOLE MILK
2 TABLESPOONS UNSWEETENED COCOA POWDER
2 TABLESPOONS SUGAR
1/4 TEASPOON VANILLA EXTRACT
WHIPPED CREAM AND CHOCOLATE SHAVINGS FOR GARNISH

RECIPE:

1. In a saucepan, heat the milk over low heat until hot but not boiling.
2. In a separate bowl, mix cocoa powder and sugar.
3. Slowly add a bit of the hot milk to the cocoa mixture, stirring until smooth.
4. Pour the cocoa mixture back into the saucepan with the milk.
5. Stir in the vanilla extract.
6. Pour into mugs and top with whipped cream and chocolate shavings.

Fun Fact: The first chocolate beverage is believed to date back to 500 BC and was made by the Mayans.

Chef Insight: For a more luxurious version, use real chocolate chunks and melt them into the milk. It'll give a richer, creamier texture.

MOJITO

INGREDIENTS:

10 FRESH MINT LEAVES, PLUS A SPRIG FOR GARNISH
1/2 LIME, CUT INTO 4 WEDGES
2 TABLESPOONS SUGAR
1 CUP ICE CUBES
1 1/2 OZ WHITE RUM
1/2 CUP CLUB SODA

RECIPE:

1. Place mint leaves and one lime wedge into a sturdy glass.
2. Use a muddler to crush the mint and lime to release the mint oils and lime juice.
3. Add two more lime wedges and the sugar, and muddle again.
4. Fill the glass with ice.
5. Pour the rum over the ice.
6. Top with club soda, stir well, and garnish with a lime wedge and sprig of mint.

Fun Fact: The Mojito has roots in a 16th-century indigenous concoction made of lime, mint, and sugar. It was later adapted into the cocktail we love today.

Chef Insight: Use fresh mint for the best aroma and flavor. The key to a great Mojito is the muddling—be gentle, so you release the oils but don't shred the leaves.

Beverages

PIÑA COLADA

INGREDIENTS:

1 1/2 OZ WHITE RUM
1 1/2 OZ COCONUT CREAM
3 OZ PINEAPPLE JUICE
PINEAPPLE SLICE AND MARASCHINO CHERRY FOR GARNISH
ICE

RECIPE:

1. Add rum, coconut cream, and pineapple juice to a blender with a scoop of ice.
2. Blend until smooth.
3. Pour into a chilled glass and garnish with a pineapple slice and maraschino cherry.

Fun Fact: The Piña Colada hails from Puerto Rico and became its official beverage in 1978.

Chef Insight: Use fresh pineapple juice if possible, as it brings a zestier, more authentic flavor to the drink.

MOSCOW MULE

INGREDIENTS:

1 1/2 OZ VODKA
1/2 OZ LIME JUICE, FRESHLY SQUEEZED
1/2 CUP GINGER BEER
LIME WEDGE AND MINT FOR GARNISH
ICE

RECIPE:

1. Fill a copper mug with ice.
2. Pour vodka and lime juice over ice.
3. Top with ginger beer.
4. Stir gently to combine.
5. Garnish with a lime wedge and a mint sprig.

Fun Fact: The Moscow Mule was invented in the 1940s to promote vodka, which was relatively unpopular in the United States at the time.

Chef Insight: The copper mug isn't just for looks; it keeps the drink colder, enhances the flavor, and amps up the fizziness of the ginger beer.

Sauces and Dips

MARINARA SAUCE

INGREDIENTS:

1 CAN (28 OZ) CRUSHED TOMATOES
1 ONION, FINELY CHOPPED
3 GARLIC CLOVES, MINCED
2 TBSP OLIVE OIL
1 TSP OREGANO
SALT AND PEPPER TO TASTE
FRESH BASIL LEAVES FOR GARNISH

RECIPE:

1. Heat olive oil in a pot over medium heat.
2. Sauté the chopped onion until translucent.
3. Add minced garlic and cook for 1-2 minutes.
4. Pour in the crushed tomatoes and add oregano.
5. Simmer for 20-30 minutes.
6. Season with salt and pepper.
7. Garnish with fresh basil leaves before serving.

Fun Fact: Marinara means "sailor-style" in Italian, and it's said the sauce was a staple among Neapolitan sailors.

Chef Insight: Adding a pinch of sugar can help balance out the acidity of the tomatoes.

Sauces and Dips

PESTO SAUCE

INGREDIENTS:

2 CUPS FRESH BASIL LEAVES
1/2 CUP GRATED PARMESAN CHEESE
1/2 CUP OLIVE OIL
1/3 CUP PINE NUTS
3 GARLIC CLOVES, MINCED
SALT AND PEPPER TO TASTE

RECIPE:

1. In a food processor, combine basil leaves, pine nuts, garlic, and grated Parmesan.
2. Pulse until finely chopped.
3. While the processor is running, slowly add the olive oil.
4. Season with salt and pepper.

Fun Fact: Pesto originates from Genoa in the Ligurian region of Italy.

Chef Insight: For a nut-free version, you can substitute pine nuts with sunflower seeds.

TZATZIKI SAUCE

INGREDIENTS:

1 CUP GREEK YOGURT
1 CUCUMBER, FINELY GRATED AND DRAINED
2 GARLIC CLOVES, MINCED
1 TBSP OLIVE OIL
1 TBSP LEMON JUICE
1 TBSP FRESH DILL, CHOPPED
SALT TO TASTE

RECIPE:

1. Combine Greek yogurt, grated cucumber, minced garlic, olive oil, and lemon juice in a bowl.
2. Stir in the chopped dill.
3. Season with salt to taste.
4. Refrigerate for at least 2 hours before serving.

Fun Fact: Tzatziki has its roots in the cuisines of Southeast Europe and the Middle East.

Chef Insight: Make sure to drain the grated cucumber well to prevent the sauce from becoming too watery.

Sauces and Dips

EASY AIOLI

INGREDIENTS:

1 CUP MAYONNAISE
3 GARLIC CLOVES, MINCED
1 TABLESPOON LEMON JUICE
SALT TO TASTE

RECIPE:

1. In a bowl, combine mayonnaise, minced garlic, and lemon juice.
2. Mix until well incorporated.
3. Season with salt to taste.

Fun Fact: In Catalonia, Spain, there is an event known as "Aioli Mon" or "Aioli Festival," where people compete to make the largest batch of aioli using a wooden pestle and mortar. The key to traditional aioli is emulsification, which can take a lot of skill (and muscle) when done by hand!

Chef Insight: Making it from scratch with egg yolks and olive oil can be rewarding, but this quick version can save you time.

ROMESCO

INGREDIENTS:

1 ROASTED RED BELL PEPPER
1 GARLIC CLOVE
1/2 CUP ALMONDS, TOASTED
1/4 CUP TOMATO PURÉE
2 TABLESPOONS OLIVE OIL
1 TABLESPOON RED WINE VINEGAR
SALT AND PEPPER TO TASTE

RECIPE:

1. In a food processor, combine the roasted red bell pepper, garlic, almonds, and tomato purée.
2. Pulse until smooth.
3. Add olive oil and red wine vinegar, then blend again.
4. Season with salt and pepper to taste.

Fun Fact: Romesco sauce hails from Tarragona, Catalonia, and is traditionally served with fish.

Chef Insight: Using hazelnuts instead of almonds will bring out a different, yet equally delicious, flavor profile.

Sauces and Dips

SALSA BRAVA

INGREDIENTS:

1 CAN (14 OZ) DICED TOMATOES
1 SMALL ONION, CHOPPED
2 GARLIC CLOVES, MINCED
1 TABLESPOON SMOKED PAPRIKA
1 TEASPOON CAYENNE PEPPER
2 TABLESPOONS OLIVE OIL
SALT TO TASTE

RECIPE:

1. Heat olive oil in a pan over medium heat.
2. Sauté onion and garlic until translucent.
3. Add the diced tomatoes, smoked paprika, and cayenne pepper.
4. Simmer for 10-15 minutes until thickened.
5. Blend to your desired consistency and season with salt.

Fun Fact: This sauce is the signature element of "Patatas Bravas," a popular Spanish tapa.

Chef Insight: Feel free to adjust the heat by adding more or less cayenne pepper.

SALSA VERDE

INGREDIENTS:

1 CUP FRESH CILANTRO LEAVES
1/2 CUP FRESH PARSLEY LEAVES
1/4 CUP FRESH MINT LEAVES
3 GARLIC CLOVES
1/4 CUP CAPERS
1 LEMON, JUICED
1/2 CUP OLIVE OIL
SALT AND PEPPER TO TASTE

RECIPE:

1. Combine cilantro, parsley, mint, garlic, capers, and lemon juice in a food processor.
2. Pulse until finely chopped.
3. Slowly add in the olive oil while the processor is running.
4. Season with salt and pepper to taste.

Fun Fact: Despite its Italian name, "Salsa Verde" variations exist in many countries, each with its unique twist.

Chef Insight: You can substitute lime juice for lemon juice for a different citrus kick.

Sauces and Dips

BARBECUE SAUCE

INGREDIENTS:

1 CUP KETCHUP
1/4 CUP APPLE CIDER VINEGAR
1/4 CUP BROWN SUGAR
1 TABLESPOON WORCESTERSHIRE SAUCE
1 TABLESPOON SMOKED PAPRIKA
1 TEASPOON GARLIC POWDER
1 TEASPOON ONION POWDER
SALT AND PEPPER TO TASTE

RECIPE:

1. Combine all ingredients in a saucepan.
2. Cook over medium heat, stirring occasionally.
3. Simmer for about 15-20 minutes until it thickens.
4. Season with salt and pepper to taste.

Fun Fact: Barbecue sauce dates back as far as the 17th century.

Chef Insight: You can infuse it with flavors like pineapple or bourbon for a more adventurous take.

HONEY MUSTARD

INGREDIENTS:

1/4 CUP HONEY
1/4 CUP DIJON MUSTARD
1 TABLESPOON WHITE WINE VINEGAR
SALT TO TASTE

RECIPE:

1. Whisk together honey, Dijon mustard, and white wine vinegar in a bowl.
2. Season with salt to taste.

Fun Fact: Honey mustard is a popular dip in the U.S but is also used globally in various forms as a dressing or marinade.

Chef Insight: Adding a pinch of cayenne can give this sweet sauce a spicy edge.

Sauces and Dips

ROASTED RED PEPPER SAUCE

INGREDIENTS:

3 RED BELL PEPPERS
2 GARLIC CLOVES, PEELED
1/4 CUP OLIVE OIL
1 TEASPOON SMOKED PAPRIKA (OPTIONAL)
SALT AND PEPPER TO TASTE
1/4 CUP GRATED PARMESAN CHEESE
1/4 CUP FRESH BASIL OR PARSLEY, CHOPPED

RECIPE:

1. Preheat your oven to 450°F (230°C). Place the red bell peppers and garlic cloves on a baking sheet.
2. Roast the peppers and garlic for 20-25 minutes, turning occasionally, until the skin is charred.
3. Remove from the oven and place the peppers in a bowl. Cover with plastic wrap or a towel and let them steam for about 10min.
4. Peel the charred skin off the peppers and remove the seeds.
5. In a blender or food processor, combine the roasted peppers, garlic, olive oil, smoked paprika (if using), salt, and pepper.
6. Blend until smooth, then stir in the grated Parmesan and herbs.

Fun Fact: The roasting process intensifies the natural sweetness of the peppers, giving the sauce a deep, rich flavor that's hard to resist.

Chef Insight: For an extra layer of complexity, you can add a splash of balsamic vinegar or a teaspoon of capers. These ingredients lend an extra layer of tanginess and depth to the sauce.

Snacks

Snacks

TRAIL MIX

INGREDIENTS:

1 CUP ALMONDS
1 CUP CASHEWS
1 CUP DRIED CRANBERRIES
1 CUP CHOCOLATE CHIPS
1 CUP MINI PRETZELS

RECIPE:

1. In a large bowl, mix all ingredients together.
2. Store in an airtight container.

Fun Fact: Trail mix was designed to be a high-energy snack for hikers and is meant to be lightweight, easy to store, and nutritious.

Chef Insight: You can tailor your trail mix according to your nutritional needs. For instance, add some pumpkin seeds for added magnesium and zinc.

HOMEMADE POPCORN

INGREDIENTS:

1/2 CUP POPCORN KERNELS
1/4 CUP VEGETABLE OIL
SALT TO TASTE

RECIPE:

1. Heat the oil in a large pot over medium heat.
2. Add three popcorn kernels as "test kernels" to judge when the oil is hot enough.
3. Once the test kernels pop, remove the pot from heat and take out the popped kernels.
4. Add the rest of the popcorn kernels and cover the pot.
5. Shake the pot occasionally and listen for the popping to slow down, then remove from heat.

Fun Fact: Popcorn is one of the oldest types of corn with evidence suggesting it's been around for thousands of years!

Chef Insight: To add some flair, try seasoning with nutritional yeast for a cheesy, vegan twist.

Snacks

VEGGIE CHIPS

INGREDIENTS:

2 SWEET POTATOES, THINLY SLICED
2 BEETS, THINLY SLICED
2 ZUCCHINIS, THINLY SLICED
OLIVE OIL
SALT TO TASTE

RECIPE:

1. Preheat oven to 375°F (190°C).
2. Toss the thinly sliced veggies in olive oil and salt.
3. Arrange on a baking sheet in a single layer.
4. Bake for 20-30 minutes or until crispy, flipping halfway through.

Fun Fact: Veggie chips can be a healthier alternative to regular chips, especially if you make them at home to control the amount of salt and oil.

Chef Insight: Using a mandoline slicer can give you consistent, thin slices for better crisping, but be careful because they are incredibly sharp.

CHOCOLATE-COVERED STRAWBERRIES

INGREDIENTS:

1 LB FRESH STRAWBERRIES, WASHED AND DRIED
8 OUNCES SEMI-SWEET CHOCOLATE
1 TABLESPOON COCONUT OIL (OPTIONAL)

RECIPE:

1. Melt the chocolate and coconut oil together using a double boiler or microwave.
2. Dip each strawberry into the melted chocolate, covering half or two-thirds of the strawberry.
3. Place the dipped strawberries on a parchment paper-lined tray.
4. Refrigerate for at least 30 minutes to let the chocolate harden.

Fun Fact: Strawberries are not actually berries in the botanical sense because their seeds are on the outside.

Chef Insight: For an extra touch, drizzle some white chocolate over the dark chocolate for a contrasting visual appeal and flavor.

Snacks

CHEESE STICKS

INGREDIENTS:

1 SHEET PUFF PASTRY, THAWED
1 CUP SHREDDED CHEDDAR CHEESE
1 EGG, BEATEN
A PINCH OF PAPRIKA OR GARLIC POWDER (OPTIONAL)

RECIPE:

1. Preheat the oven to 400°F (200°C).
2. Roll out the puff pastry and sprinkle the cheddar cheese on top.
3. Fold the pastry over the cheese and use a rolling pin to seal it in.
4. Cut into 1-inch wide strips.
5. Twist each strip and place on a lined baking sheet.
6. Brush with beaten egg and sprinkle with paprika or garlic powder if using.
7. Bake for 10-12 minutes or until golden brown.

Fun Fact: Puff pastry was invented in France and is known for its light, flaky layers.

Chef Insight: Cheese sticks are a canvas for flavors. Feel free to add herbs like rosemary or thyme to the cheese mix for an aromatic twist.

RICE KRISPIES TREATS

INGREDIENTS:

3 TABLESPOONS BUTTER
4 CUPS MINI MARSHMALLOWS
6 CUPS RICE KRISPIES CEREAL

RECIPE:

1. Melt the butter in a large saucepan over low heat.
2. Add the marshmallows and stir until melted.
3. Remove from heat and stir in the Rice Krispies cereal until well coated.
4. Press the mixture into a greased 9x13-inch pan.
5. Let cool and cut into squares.

Fun Fact: The original recipe for Rice Krispies Treats was developed in 1939 as a fundraising idea for a Camp Fire Girls group.

Chef Insight: For a more adult version, you could add a splash of vanilla extract or a sprinkle of sea salt to the marshmallow mixture.

Snacks

PRETZELS

INGREDIENTS:

1 AND 1/2 CUPS WARM WATER
1 PACKET ACTIVE DRY YEAST
4 CUPS ALL-PURPOSE FLOUR
1 TABLESPOON SUGAR
1 TEASPOON SALT
1 EGG, BEATEN
COARSE SEA SALT FOR TOPPING

RECIPE:

1. Combine warm water and yeast in a bowl and let sit for 5 minutes.
2. Mix in the flour, sugar, and salt.
3. Knead the dough for about 7 minutes, until smooth.
4. Preheat oven to 450°F (232°C).
5. Divide dough into 12 pieces and shape into pretzels.
6. Brush with beaten egg and sprinkle with coarse sea salt.
7. Bake for 10-12 minutes until golden brown.

Fun Fact: Pretzels have religious origins; they were created by monks to resemble arms crossed in prayer.

Chef Insight: For a twist, consider sprinkling your pretzels with some cinnamon sugar instead of salt for a sweet treat!

GRANOLA BARS

INGREDIENTS:

2 CUPS OLD-FASHIONED OATS
1 CUP ALMONDS, CHOPPED
1/2 CUP HONEY OR MAPLE SYRUP
1/2 CUP DRIED FRUIT (RAISINS, CRANBERRIES, ETC.)
1/2 TEASPOON VANILLA EXTRACT
A PINCH OF SALT

RECIPE:

1. Preheat oven to 350°F (175°C).
2. Toast oats and almonds for 10 minutes.
3. In a large bowl, mix toasted oats and almonds with honey, dried fruit, vanilla extract, and a pinch of salt.
4. Press the mixture into a greased 8x8-inch pan.
5. Bake for 20-25 minutes.
6. Allow to cool before cutting into bars.

Fun Fact: Granola was invented in the United States and was originally a health food consisting of whole-grain products.

Chef Insight: You can add in various seeds, like pumpkin or chia seeds, for extra nutrients and crunch.

Snacks

MIXED NUTS

INGREDIENTS:

2 CUPS MIXED NUTS (ALMONDS, CASHEWS, WALNUTS, ETC.)
1 TABLESPOON OLIVE OIL
A PINCH OF SEA SALT
OPTIONAL SEASONINGS: PAPRIKA, GARLIC POWDER, OR CAYENNE PEPPER

RECIPE:

1. Preheat oven to 350°F (175°C).
2. In a bowl, mix nuts, olive oil, sea salt, and optional seasonings.
3. Spread the mixture on a baking sheet in a single layer.
4. Roast for 10-15 minutes, stirring halfway through.

Fun Fact: Nuts are a rich source of protein and good fats, making them a perfect energy-boosting snack.

Chef Insight: Roasting your own mixed nuts allows you to control the sodium and seasoning. Feel free to get creative with spices!

Beyond Instant Noodles. 200 Quick & Easy College Recipes

PISTACHIO GRANOLA

INGREDIENTS:

3 CUPS ROLLED OATS
1 CUP SHELLED PISTACHIOS, ROUGHLY CHOPPED
1/2 CUP SLIVERED ALMONDS
1/4 CUP SUNFLOWER SEEDS
1/2 CUP HONEY OR MAPLE SYRUP
1/4 CUP COCONUT OIL, MELTED
1 TEASPOON VANILLA EXTRACT
1/2 TEASPOON CINNAMON

RECIPE:

1. Preheat your oven to 325°F (160°C). Line a baking sheet with parchment paper.
2. In a large mixing bowl, combine rolled oats, chopped pistachios, slivered almonds, and sunflower seeds.
3. In a separate bowl, whisk together honey, melted coconut oil, vanilla extract, and cinnamon. Optional: add a pinch of salt
4. Pour the wet mixture over the dry ingredients and mix well.
5. Spread the mixture evenly on the prepared baking sheet.
6. Bake for 20-25', stirring halfway through, until golden brown.
7. Remove from the oven and let it cool completely. It will become crunchier as it cools.

Fun Fact: Pistachios are one of the oldest flowering nut trees, and humans have been eating them for at least 9,000 years!

Chef Insight: Make sure to let the granola cool completely before storing it in an airtight container. This ensures it stays crunchy for a longer period.

Asian Cuisine

PAD THAI

INGREDIENTS:

8 OZ RICE NOODLES
2 TABLESPOONS VEGETABLE OIL
1/2 CUP TOFU, DICED
1 EGG
1 CUP BEAN SPROUTS
2 GREEN ONIONS, CHOPPED

SAUCE:

2 TABLESPOONS TAMARIND PASTE
1 TABLESPOON FISH SAUCE
1 TABLESPOON SUGAR

RECIPE:

1. Prepare rice noodles according to package instructions.
2. In a wok, heat oil and sauté tofu until golden.
3. Push tofu aside and scramble the egg in the wok.
4. Add noodles and sauce, mixing well.
5. Fold in bean sprouts and green onions.
6. Serve with lime wedges and crushed peanuts.

Fun Fact: Pad Thai was popularized during WWII as a part of a government campaign to promote nationalism in Thailand.

Chef Insights: Soaking the rice noodles in warm water instead of boiling them prevents them from becoming too mushy. Tamarind paste is the key to authentic Pad Thai flavor. Don't skip it!

Asian cuisine

SUSHI

INGREDIENTS:

**2 CUPS SUSHI RICE
1/4 CUP RICE VINEGAR
1/2 POUND FRESH SUSHI-GRADE FISH
1 AVOCADO, SLICED
1 CUCUMBER, SLICED
NORI SHEETS**

RECIPE:

1. Rinse and cook sushi rice according to package instructions.
2. Once cooked, season with rice vinegar.
3. Slice fish into thin pieces.
4. Place a bamboo sushi rolling mat inside a gallon-size Ziploc bag.
5. Place a sheet of plastic wrap on top of the mat, then a sheet of nori.
6. Spread a layer of rice on the nori, leaving a small border around the edges.
7. Place fish, avocado, and cucumber in the center.
8. Roll tightly using the bamboo mat.
9. Cut into bite-sized pieces and serve with soy sauce and wasabi.

Fun Fact: The sushi we're familiar with is known as "Edo-mae sushi," which originated as fast food in Tokyo in the 19th century.

Chef Insights: Always use sushi-grade fish for making sushi at home. Sushi rice should be sticky but not mushy; the vinegar seasoning helps with this texture.

SPRING ROLLS

INGREDIENTS:

RICE PAPER SHEETS
1 CUP COOKED SHRIMP, PEELED AND HALVED
1 CUP LETTUCE, SHREDDED
1/2 CUP CARROTS, JULIENNED
1/2 CUP CUCUMBER, JULIENNED
FRESH MINT AND CILANTRO LEAVES

RECIPE:

1. Soak rice paper sheets in warm water until pliable.
2. Lay out the soaked rice paper, and place a small amount of each ingredient in the center.
3. Fold in the sides and roll tightly.
4. Serve with a dipping sauce of your choice (like hoisin or peanut sauce).

Fun Fact: Spring rolls can be found in various Asian cuisines, and they can be served fried or fresh.

Chef Insights: You can replace shrimp with tofu for a vegetarian option. Rolling takes practice! Don't overstuff the rolls to make the process easier.

Asian cuisine

TERIYAKI CHICKEN

INGREDIENTS:

2 CHICKEN BREASTS, CUT INTO BITE-SIZE PIECES
1 TABLESPOON VEGETABLE OIL

SAUCE:

1/4 CUP SOY SAUCE
1/4 CUP MIRIN
2 TABLESPOONS SUGAR
1 CLOVE GARLIC, MINCED
1 TEASPOON GINGER, GRATED

RECIPE:

1. Heat oil in a pan over medium heat.
2. Add chicken pieces and cook until browned.
3. In a bowl, mix together the sauce ingredients.
4. Pour the sauce over the chicken and simmer until it thickens.
5. Serve over steamed rice with sesame seeds and chopped green onions.

Fun Fact: "Teriyaki" refers to the cooking method: "Teri" means luster, which you get from the sauce, and "yaki" means to grill or broil.

Chef Insights: Using boneless, skinless chicken thighs can make for juicier, more flavorful meat. The sauce is versatile and can be used with other proteins like fish or beef.

MISO RAMEN

INGREDIENTS:

2 PACKS RAMEN NOODLES
4 CUPS CHICKEN OR VEGETABLE BROTH
2 TABLESPOONS MISO PASTE
1 TABLESPOON SOY SAUCE
1 TEASPOON SESAME OIL
1 CLOVE GARLIC, MINCED
1 TEASPOON GRATED GINGER
TOPPINGS: SLICED GREEN ONIONS, BOILED EGG, NORI, CORN, SPINACH

RECIPE:

1. Prepare ramen noodles according to package instructions and set aside.
2. In a pot, bring the broth to a simmer.
3. In a separate bowl, mix miso paste with a small amount of hot broth to dissolve it.
4. Add the miso mixture, soy sauce, sesame oil, garlic, and ginger to the pot.
5. Simmer for 5 minutes to let the flavors meld.
6. Divide the noodles between bowls and pour the broth over them.
7. Add your choice of toppings.

Fun Fact: Miso paste is fermented soybean paste and has been a staple in Japanese cooking for over a thousand years.

Chef Insights: Using different types of miso (red, white, or mixed) can greatly affect the flavor profile. The toppings are where you can get creative; traditional toppings include bamboo shoots, chashu pork, and bean sprouts.

Asian cuisine

BAO BUNS

INGREDIENTS:

1 CUP WARM MILK
2 TEASPOONS ACTIVE DRY YEAST
3 CUPS ALL-PURPOSE FLOUR
1/4 CUP SUGAR
1 TEASPOON BAKING POWDER

FILLING:

1 LB PORK BELLY, SLICED
1/4 CUP HOISIN SAUCE
1 TABLESPOON SOY SAUCE
1 TABLESPOON HONEY
1 TEASPOON FIVE-SPICE POWDER

RECIPE:

1. Mix warm milk and yeast. Let sit for 10 minutes.
2. Combine flour, sugar, and baking powder. Add the yeast mixture and knead until smooth.
3. Let the dough rise for 1 hour or until doubled.
4. For the filling, marinate pork belly in hoisin sauce, soy sauce, honey, and five-spice powder.
5. Cook pork belly until tender and caramelized.
6. Divide the dough into small balls and flatten them into disks.
7. Add a slice of pork belly in the center and fold the dough over, pinching to seal.
8. Steam buns for 15 minutes.

Fun Fact: Bao buns are also known as "Hirata buns" in some parts of the world, named after the Taiwanese chef who popularized them in New York.

Chef Insights: Ensure your milk isn't too hot; otherwise, you'll kill the yeast. Feel free to add pickled vegetables or fresh cilantro as additional fillings for added texture and flavor.

DUMPLINGS

INGREDIENTS:

2 CUPS ALL-PURPOSE FLOUR
1 CUP BOILING WATER

FILLING:

1 LB GROUND PORK
1/2 CUP MINCED CABBAGE
1/4 CUP CHOPPED GREEN ONIONS
1 TABLESPOON SOY SAUCE
1 TEASPOON SESAME OIL
1 CLOVE GARLIC, MINCED
SALT AND PEPPER TO TASTE

RECIPE:

1. For the dough, mix flour and boiling water until a dough forms. Knead until smooth. Let it rest for 30 minutes.
2. Combine all filling ingredients in a bowl.
3. Roll out dough into small circles.
4. Place a spoonful of filling in the center of each circle.
5. Fold and seal the dumplings.
6. Steam or boil until the pork is cooked through, about 15 minutes.

Fun Fact: Dumplings are a universal concept, appearing in various forms in cuisines all over the world, from Italian ravioli to Japanese gyoza.

Chef Insights: You can substitute the pork with chicken, shrimp, or even a vegetarian mix. Different folding techniques can be used for aesthetic purposes as well as for differentiation of fillings.

Asian cuisine

KUNG PAO CHICKEN

INGREDIENTS:

1 LB BONELESS CHICKEN BREASTS, CUBED
1 TABLESPOON SOY SAUCE
1 TABLESPOON CORNSTARCH
2 TABLESPOONS VEGETABLE OIL
1/2 CUP PEANUTS OR CASHEWS
1 RED BELL PEPPER, DICED

2 CLOVES GARLIC, MINCED
1 TEASPOON MINCED GINGER
2 TABLESPOONS HOISIN SAUCE
1 TABLESPOON VINEGAR
1 TEASPOON SUGAR
RED PEPPER FLAKES TO TASTE

RECIPE:

1. Marinate chicken in soy sauce and cornstarch for 30 minutes.
2. Heat oil in a wok or large skillet. Sauté peanuts or cashews until golden. Remove and set aside.
3. In the same oil, cook chicken until browned and cooked through. Remove and set aside.
4. Stir-fry red bell pepper, garlic, and ginger until fragrant.
5. Add hoisin sauce, vinegar, and sugar. Add red pepper flakes to taste.
6. Add the chicken back into the wok, stir to coat with sauce.
7. Add peanuts or cashews, mix well and serve.

Fun Fact: Kung Pao Chicken is named after a Qing Dynasty official. The dish was his favorite, and so it carries his title: Kung Pao (or Gong Bao).

Chef Insights: Feel free to add more vegetables like zucchini or snap peas. The peanuts or cashews provide a delightful crunch that contrasts with the tender chicken, so don't skip them!

TEMPURA

INGREDIENTS:

1 CUP ALL-PURPOSE FLOUR
1 EGG
1 CUP COLD SPARKLING WATER
1 TEASPOON SALT
ASSORTED VEGETABLES (BELL PEPPERS, SWEET POTATOES, MUSHROOMS, ETC.)
ASSORTED SEAFOOD (SHRIMP, SQUID, ETC.)
OIL FOR FRYING

RECIPE:

1. Whisk together flour, egg, sparkling water, and salt to create the batter.
2. Heat oil to 350°F (175°C).
3. Dip the vegetables and seafood into the batter, making sure they're fully coated.
4. Fry in batches until golden, about 2-3 minutes.
5. Drain on a paper towel and serve immediately.

Fun Fact: Tempura has Portuguese origins. It was introduced to Japan by Portuguese missionaries and traders in the 16th century.

Chef Insights: The key to a light, crispy tempura is cold batter and hot oil. You can use beer instead of sparkling water for a slightly different flavor profile.

Asian cuisine

KOREAN BEEF AND RICE

INGREDIENTS:

1 1/2 POUNDS SIRLOIN BEEF STRIPS
1/2 CUP BEEF BROTH
1/4 CUP SOY SAUCE
1/4 CUP BROWN SUGAR
1 TABLESPOON SESAME OIL
4 CLOVES GARLIC, MINCED
1 TEASPOON FRESH GRATED GINGER
1 TABLESPOON CORNSTARCH
2 TABLESPOONS COLD WATER
SLICED GREEN ONIONS AND SESAME SEEDS FOR GARNISH

RECIPE:

1. Add the beef, beef broth, soy sauce, brown sugar, sesame oil, garlic, and ginger into the pressure cooker. Cook for 20 min.
2. Once done, open the pressure cooker safely.
3. In a separate bowl, mix cornstarch and cold water until smooth.
4. Heat the opened pot over medium-high heat, and stir in the cornstarch mixture. Cook until the sauce has thickened.
5. Garnish with sliced green onions and sesame seeds before serving.

Fun Fact: Pressure cookers have been a game-changer in modern cooking, offering a multitude of cooking functions and reducing cooking time significantly.

Chef Insights: Make sure to cut the beef into even pieces for uniform cooking. Feel free to add vegetables like bell peppers or carrots to add extra nutrition and color to the dish.

European Cuisine

SHEPHERD'S PIE

INGREDIENTS:

1 LB GROUND LAMB
1 ONION, CHOPPED
1 CUP MIXED VEGETABLES (PEAS, CARROTS, CORN)
2 CUPS MASHED POTATOES
1 CUP BEEF BROTH
SALT AND PEPPER TO TASTE

RECIPE:

1. Preheat oven to 400°F (200°C).
2. In a skillet, cook ground lamb and onion until browned. Drain excess fat.
3. Add mixed vegetables and beef broth. Simmer until thickened.
4. Transfer to a baking dish and top with mashed potatoes.
5. Bake for 20 minutes or until golden brown.

Fun Fact: Shepherd's Pie is traditionally made with lamb, while its beef counterpart is usually called "Cottage Pie."

Chef Insights: Using freshly mashed potatoes instead of instant ones will significantly improve the dish.

European cuisine

FRENCH ONION SOUP

INGREDIENTS:

4 LARGE ONIONS, THINLY SLICED
4 CUPS BEEF BROTH
2 CUPS GRATED GRUYÈRE CHEESE
4 SLICES OF BAGUETTE
2 TABLESPOONS BUTTER
SALT AND PEPPER TO TASTE

RECIPE:

1. Melt butter in a pot and add onions. Cook until caramelized.
2. Add beef broth and simmer for 20 minutes. Season with salt and pepper.
3. Preheat broiler. Ladle soup into oven-safe bowls, top with a slice of baguette and sprinkle with cheese.
4. Broil until cheese is bubbly and golden.

Fun Fact: French Onion Soup dates back to Roman times, though the modern version originated in France.

Chef Insights: The key to a great French Onion Soup is the caramelization of the onions; don't rush this step.

PULPO A LA GALLEGA

INGREDIENTS:

1 LB OCTOPUS
4 POTATOES, SLICED
1 TEASPOON SMOKED PAPRIKA
SALT AND OLIVE OIL

RECIPE:

1. Boil the octopus until tender, about 45 minutes. Cut into bite-sized pieces.
2. Boil the potatoes until tender.
3. Arrange octopus and potatoes on a platter.
4. Drizzle with olive oil, sprinkle with paprika and salt.

Fun Fact: This dish is a staple in Galician cuisine and is traditionally served on wooden platters.

Chef Insights: Make sure to "frighten" the octopus before boiling it, which means dipping it into boiling water three times before fully submerging it. This helps tenderize the meat.

European cuisine

OSSO BUCO

INGREDIENTS:

4 VEAL SHANKS
1 ONION, CHOPPED
1 CARROT, CHOPPED
1 CELERY STALK, CHOPPED
2 CUPS BEEF BROTH
1 CUP WHITE WINE
2 CANS OF DICED TOMATOES
2 CLOVES GARLIC, MINCED
OLIVE OIL, SALT, AND PEPPER

RECIPE:

1. In a heavy skillet, heat olive oil. Season the veal shanks with salt and pepper and brown them on both sides. Remove and set aside.
2. In the same skillet, sauté onion, carrot, and celery until softened.
3. Add garlic, then deglaze with white wine.
4. Add beef broth and canned tomatoes. Return the veal shanks to the skillet.
5. Cover and simmer for about 1.5 hours or until meat is tender.

Fun Fact: "Osso Buco" literally means "bone hole" in Italian, referencing the marrow-filled bone in the dish.

Chef Insights: You can make a gremolata (lemon zest, garlic, and parsley) to sprinkle on top for a fresh contrast.

SALMOREJO

INGREDIENTS:

6 RIPE TOMATOES, ROUGHLY CHOPPED
1 LOAF OF BREAD (SOFT)
1 CLOVE GARLIC
1/2 CUP EXTRA VIRGIN OLIVE OIL
2 TBSP SHERRY VINEGAR
SALT TO TASTE
HARD-BOILED EGGS AND JAMÓN SERRANO FOR GARNISH

RECIPE:

1. In a blender, add the tomatoes, bread, garlic, sherry vinegar, and a pinch of salt.
2. Blend until you achieve a smooth texture.
3. While blending, slowly add the olive oil to emulsify the mixture.
4. Chill in the fridge for at least one hour.
5. Serve cold, garnished with diced hard-boiled eggs and thin slices of jamón serrano.

Fun Fact: Salmorejo originated in Andalusia, southern Spain, and was traditionally made using a mortar and pestle!

Chef Insights: This dish is all about texture. Make sure your bread is sufficiently softened and your tomatoes are ripe for maximum flavor. The quality of your olive oil can make or break this dish. Choose a high-quality extra virgin olive oil for the best results.

European cuisine

GAMBAS AL AJILLO

INGREDIENTS:

1 LB SHRIMP, PEELED AND DEVEINED
5 CLOVES GARLIC, THINLY SLICED
1/2 CUP OLIVE OIL
1/4 TEASPOON RED PEPPER FLAKES
SALT AND LEMON JUICE TO TASTE

RECIPE:

1. Heat olive oil in a skillet over medium heat.
2. Add the garlic and red pepper flakes. Cook until garlic is lightly golden.
3. Add shrimp and cook until pink, about 2 minutes per side.
4. Season with salt and a splash of lemon juice.

Fun Fact: "Gambas al Ajillo" is a popular tapas dish in Spain, especially in the Andalusian region.

Chef Insights: Always use the freshest shrimp you can find; frozen shrimp often has a less delicate flavor.

MOUSSAKA

INGREDIENTS:

2 LARGE EGGPLANTS, SLICED
1 LB GROUND LAMB
1 ONION, CHOPPED
2 CLOVES GARLIC, MINCED
1 CAN DICED TOMATOES
1 TSP CINNAMON 1 TSP OREGANO
OLIVE OIL, SALT, AND PEPPER

FOR THE BECHAMEL:

2 CUPS MILK
4 TBSP BUTTER
4 TBSP FLOUR
NUTMEG
SALT

RECIPE:

1. Salt the eggplant slices and let them drain for 30 minutes. Rinse and pat dry.
2. Sauté the eggplant slices in olive oil until browned. Set aside.
3. In the same pan, brown the ground lamb. Add onions and garlic and cook until softened.
4. Add tomatoes, cinnamon, and oregano. Simmer for 20 minutes.
5. Make the bechamel by melting butter, adding flour, and gradually whisking in milk. Season with nutmeg and salt.
6. Layer a baking dish with eggplant, meat sauce, and bechamel. Repeat.
7. Bake at 350°F (175°C) for 45 minutes.

Fun Fact: Moussaka is common in the Balkans and Middle East but is most famous in Greece.

Chef Insights: Draining the eggplant helps to remove any bitterness and allows it to absorb the flavors better.

European cuisine

GOULASH

INGREDIENTS:

2 LBS BEEF STEW MEAT, CUBED
2 ONIONS, CHOPPED
2 BELL PEPPERS, DICED
3 CLOVES GARLIC, MINCED
2 TBSP PAPRIKA
4 CUPS BEEF BROTH
1 CAN DICED TOMATOES
OLIVE OIL, SALT, AND PEPPER

RECIPE:

1. Heat oil in a pot, brown the beef cubes, and set aside.
2. In the same pot, sauté onions until translucent.
3. Add garlic and bell peppers, then stir in the paprika.
4. Return the beef to the pot, add beef broth and tomatoes.
5. Simmer for about 2 hours or until the meat is tender.

Fun Fact: Goulash originated as a shepherd's dish in Hungary.

Chef Insights: Use authentic Hungarian paprika for a richer flavor and deeper color.

HUEVOS ROTOS

INGREDIENTS:

4 LARGE EGGS
4 MEDIUM POTATOES, THINLY SLICED
SPANISH CHORIZO, SLICED (OPTIONAL)
OLIVE OIL, SALT

RECIPE:

1. Deep-fry the potato slices until golden. Drain and set aside.
2. Combine potatoes with chorizo if using.
3. In a skillet, fry the eggs until the whites are set but yolks are still runny.
4. Place the eggs over the potato mixture and break the yolks before serving.

Fun Fact: "Huevos Rotos" literally means "broken eggs" in Spanish, and it's a beloved comfort food.

Chef Insights: Use high-quality olive oil for frying for the best flavor profile.

European cuisine

CHATEAUBRIAND

INGREDIENTS:

1 CHATEAUBRIAND CUT OF BEEF (ABOUT 1-1.5 LBS)
2 TBSP OLIVE OIL
SALT AND PEPPER TO TASTE
3 TBSP BUTTER
3 CLOVES GARLIC, MINCED
2 SPRIGS FRESH THYME
2 SPRIGS FRESH ROSEMARY

RECIPE:

1. Preheat your oven to 425°F (220°C).
2. Season the beef with salt and pepper.
3. Heat olive oil in an oven-safe skillet over high heat. Sear each side of the beef for 1-2 minutes.
4. Add butter, garlic, thyme, and rosemary to the skillet.
5. Transfer the skillet to the oven and roast for 10-15 minutes for medium-rare.
6. Let rest for 5 minutes before slicing.

Fun Fact: Chateaubriand is named after a French viscount who was a diplomat and writer, not a chef!

Chef Insights: Using an oven-safe skillet lets you go from stove-top to oven seamlessly, retaining all those delicious juices and flavors.

Middle Eastern Cuisine

Middle Eastern cuisine

SHAWARMA

INGREDIENTS:

1 LB BONELESS CHICKEN THIGHS
2 TBSP OLIVE OIL
1 TBSP CUMIN
1 TBSP PAPRIKA
1 TSP TURMERIC
1 TSP GARLIC POWDER
SALT AND PEPPER TO TASTE
PITA BREAD AND FRESH VEGGIES FOR SERVING

RECIPE:

1. In a bowl, combine olive oil, cumin, paprika, turmeric, and garlic powder.
2. Add chicken thighs and marinate for at least 2 hours or overnight.
3. Preheat grill or skillet over medium-high heat.
4. Cook the chicken until fully cooked, about 5-7 minutes per side.
5. Slice and serve with pita and fresh veggies.

Fun Fact: Shawarma is believed to have originated from the Ottoman Empire and was originally made with lamb.

Chef Insights: Marinating the chicken overnight allows the spices to penetrate more deeply, leading to a more flavorful result.

HUMMUS

INGREDIENTS:

1 CAN CHICKPEAS, DRAINED AND RINSED
1/4 CUP TAHINI
2 CLOVES GARLIC
3 TBSP LEMON JUICE
2 TBSP OLIVE OIL
SALT TO TASTE
PAPRIKA AND ADDITIONAL OLIVE OIL FOR GARNISH

RECIPE:

1. In a food processor, add chickpeas, tahini, garlic, lemon juice, olive oil, and salt.
2. Blend until smooth, adding water as needed for desired consistency.
3. Garnish with paprika and a drizzle of olive oil before serving.

Fun Fact: Hummus means "chickpea" in Arabic.

Chef Insights: Using cold ingredients can affect the texture of the hummus. Room temperature ingredients blend more effectively.

Middle Eastern cuisine

FALAFEL

INGREDIENTS:

1 CUP DRIED CHICKPEAS
1/2 LARGE ONION, CHOPPED
2 CLOVES GARLIC, MINCED
2 TBSP FRESH PARSLEY, CHOPPED
1 TBSP GROUND CUMIN
1 TSP GROUND CORIANDER
SALT AND PEPPER TO TASTE
OIL FOR FRYING

RECIPE:

1. Soak chickpeas in water for at least 8 hours or overnight. Drain and rinse.
2. In a food processor, add soaked chickpeas, onion, garlic, parsley, cumin, coriander, salt, and pepper.
3. Pulse until the mixture is coarse and holds together.
4. Form into small patties.
5. Heat oil in a deep pan and fry the patties until golden brown, about 4-5 minutes each side.

Fun Fact: Falafel was originally made with fava beans and has been enjoyed in the Middle East for over a thousand years!

Chef Insights: Do not use canned chickpeas; the texture won't be the same. Soaking dried chickpeas gives you that perfect, crispy falafel exterior.

KOFTA

INGREDIENTS:

1 LB GROUND BEEF OR LAMB
1 ONION, GRATED
2 CLOVES GARLIC, MINCED
1/4 CUP FRESH PARSLEY, CHOPPED
1 TSP GROUND CUMIN
1/2 TSP GROUND CINNAMON
SALT AND PEPPER TO TASTE

RECIPE:

1. In a bowl, combine ground meat, onion, garlic, parsley, cumin, cinnamon, salt, and pepper.
2. Mix well and form into elongated, sausage-like shapes.
3. Preheat grill or skillet to medium-high heat.
4. Cook the kofta until fully cooked, turning occasionally, about 6-8 minutes.

Fun Fact: Kofta is a versatile dish that's made with different kinds of meat and spices depending on the country it's made in.

Chef Insights: Using a combination of beef and lamb can give you an interesting blend of flavors in your kofta.

Middle Eastern cuisine

TABOULEH

INGREDIENTS:

1 CUP BULGUR WHEAT
1 1/2 CUPS BOILING WATER
1 1/2 CUPS FRESH PARSLEY, FINELY CHOPPED
3/4 CUP FRESH MINT, FINELY CHOPPED
1 CUCUMBER, DICED
3 TOMATOES, DICED
JUICE OF 1 LEMON
1/4 CUP OLIVE OIL
SALT AND PEPPER TO TASTE

RECIPE:

1. Pour boiling water over bulgur wheat in a bowl. Cover and let it sit for 30 minutes, or until softened. Drain excess water.
2. In a large bowl, combine parsley, mint, cucumber, and tomatoes.
3. Add the soaked and drained bulgur wheat to the vegetable mixture.
4. Drizzle with lemon juice and olive oil. Season with salt and pepper.
5. Toss to combine and let it chill for at least one hour before serving.

Fun Fact: Tabouleh originally comes from the mountains of Lebanon and Syria and was traditionally eaten by farmers.

Chef Insights: The key to a great tabouleh is finely chopping your herbs; this releases their oils and flavors more effectively.

193

BABA GANOUSH

INGREDIENTS:

2 MEDIUM EGGPLANTS
3 CLOVES GARLIC, MINCED
1/4 CUP TAHINI
JUICE OF 1 LEMON
2 TBSP OLIVE OIL
1/2 TSP GROUND CUMIN
SALT AND PEPPER TO TASTE
GARNISH: FRESH PARSLEY, POMEGRANATE SEEDS (OPTIONAL)

RECIPE:

1. Preheat oven to 400°F (200°C).
2. Prick the eggplants all over with a fork and roast in the oven for 35-40 minutes, until soft and skin is charred.
3. Allow the eggplants to cool, then peel and discard the skin.
4. In a food processor, combine the roasted eggplant, garlic, tahini, lemon juice, olive oil, cumin, salt, and pepper.
5. Blend until smooth, and garnish with parsley and optional pomegranate seeds before serving.

Fun Fact: Baba Ganoush is named after a sulky man (baba) in Arabic folklore who made this dish for his daughter.

Chef Insights: Roasting the eggplants until their skin chars gives the baba ganoush its distinctive smoky flavor.

Middle Eastern cuisine

LAMB MEATBALLS

INGREDIENTS:

1 LB GROUND LAMB
1 SMALL ONION, FINELY GRATED
3 CLOVES GARLIC, MINCED
1/4 CUP FRESH PARSLEY, CHOPPED
1 TEASPOON GROUND CUMIN
1 TEASPOON GROUND CORIANDER

1/2 TEASPOON GROUND CINNAMON
1/2 TEASPOON GROUND ALLSPICE
SALT AND PEPPER TO TASTE
1 EGG, BEATEN
1/2 CUP BREADCRUMBS
2 TABLESPOONS OLIVE OIL

RECIPE:

1. Preheat your oven to 400°F (200°C).
2. In a large bowl, combine ground lamb, grated onion, garlic, parsley, and spices.
3. Add the beaten egg and breadcrumbs to the mixture. Mix until well combined.
4. Shape the mixture into 1.5-inch meatballs.
5. Heat olive oil in a large skillet over medium-high heat.
6. Brown the meatballs on all sides, about 2-3 minutes per side.
7. Transfer the meatballs to a baking sheet and bake for 10-12 minutes, or until cooked through.

Fun Fact: In Middle Eastern cuisine, these meatballs are often called "kefta" or "kofte" and are typically served with a side of mint yogurt sauce or tahini.

Chef Insights: Grating the onion will give the meatballs a smoother texture and allow the flavors to meld better. The spices can be adjusted according to your personal preference.

LAMB TAGINE

INGREDIENTS:

2 LBS LAMB, CUT INTO 2-INCH CUBES
1 ONION, FINELY CHOPPED
3 CLOVES GARLIC, MINCED
1 TEASPOON GROUND CUMIN
1 TEASPOON GROUND CORIANDER
1 TEASPOON PAPRIKA
2 TEASPOONS GROUND CINNAMON

SALT AND PEPPER TO TASTE
1 CAN CHICKPEAS, DRAINED
1 CUP DRIED APRICOTS, HALVED
4 CUPS CHICKEN OR VEGETABLE BROTH
2 TABLESPOONS OLIVE OIL
FRESH CILANTRO FOR GARNISH

RECIPE:

1. In a large bowl, mix lamb with spices, salt, and pepper. Let marinate for at least 2 hours.
2. In a tagine or heavy-bottomed pot, heat olive oil over medium heat.
3. Brown the lamb on all sides. Remove and set aside.
4. In the same pot, sauté onion and garlic until translucent.
5. Return the lamb to the pot, add chickpeas, apricots, and broth.
6. Cover and simmer for 2 hours, or until lamb is tender.
7. Garnish with fresh cilantro before serving.

Fun Fact: Tagines are both the conical clay pots and the dishes cooked in them.

Chef Insights: A traditional tagine pot will give you the most authentic flavor, but a Dutch oven or a heavy-bottomed pot will also work well.

Middle Eastern cuisine

KEBABS

INGREDIENTS:

1 LB BEEF OR LAMB, CUT INTO 1-INCH CUBES
1 MEDIUM ONION, GRATED
2 CLOVES GARLIC, MINCED
1/4 CUP OLIVE OIL
JUICE OF 1 LEMON
1 TEASPOON GROUND CUMIN
1 TEASPOON PAPRIKA
SALT AND PEPPER TO TASTE
WOODEN OR METAL SKEWERS

RECIPE:

1. Combine all the ingredients except the meat in a bowl to make the marinade.
2. Add the meat cubes to the marinade, ensuring all pieces are well-coated.
3. Cover and refrigerate for at least 2 hours, preferably overnight.
4. Preheat your grill or grill pan over medium-high heat.
5. Thread the marinated meat onto skewers.
6. Grill for 8-10 minutes, turning occasionally, until cooked to your desired level.

Fun Fact: The word 'kebab' originally comes from the Arabic 'kabāb', meaning 'to burn' or 'to roast'.

Chef Insights: If using wooden skewers, soak them in water for 30 minutes before using to prevent burning. You can add vegetables like bell peppers and onions between the meat pieces for extra flavor and color.

BAKLAVA

INGREDIENTS:

16 OZ PHYLLO DOUGH, THAWED
1 CUP MELTED UNSALTED BUTTER
2 CUPS MIXED NUTS (WALNUTS,
ALMONDS, PISTACHIOS), FINELY
CHOPPED

1 CUP GRANULATED SUGAR
1 TEASPOON GROUND CINNAMON
1 CUP WATER
1 CUP HONEY

RECIPE:

1. Preheat your oven to 350°F (175°C).
2. Brush a 9x13-inch baking pan with melted butter.
3. Layer phyllo sheets in the pan, brushing each sheet with melted butter.
4. After 8 layers, sprinkle a portion of the mixed nuts.
5. Continue layering, adding nuts every 8 sheets, until all sheets are used.
6. Cut the layered dough into diamond or square shapes.
7. Bake for 45-50 minutes until golden brown.
8. While the baklava is baking, make the syrup by boiling sugar, water, and honey together. Simmer for 10 minutes.
9. Pour the syrup over the baklava as soon as it comes out of the oven.

Fun Fact: Baklava has a long history and is claimed by many Middle Eastern and Mediterranean countries, but its exact origins are still a sweet mystery.

Chef Insights: Make sure to cover the phyllo dough with a damp towel while working to prevent it from drying out.

Latin Cuisine

REINA PEPIADA

INGREDIENTS:

2 RIPE AVOCADOS
2 CUPS SHREDDED COOKED CHICKEN
1/4 CUP MAYONNAISE
1/4 CUP CHOPPED CILANTRO
JUICE OF 1 LIME
SALT AND PEPPER TO TASTE
4 AREPAS

RECIPE:

1. Mash the avocados in a bowl.
2. Add shredded chicken, mayonnaise, cilantro, and lime juice. Mix well.
3. Season with salt and pepper.
4. Cut open the arepas and stuff them with the chicken and avocado mixture.

Fun Fact: The name "Reina Pepiada" comes from a Venezuelan beauty queen; it roughly translates to "Curvy Queen."

Chef Insights: The quality of the avocados matters a lot. Choose ripe but firm avocados for the best texture and flavor. For a better result, use a rotisserie chicken.

Latin cuisine

EMPANADAS

INGREDIENTS:

1 LB GROUND BEEF
1 ONION, FINELY CHOPPED
2 CLOVES GARLIC, MINCED
1 TEASPOON CUMIN
SALT AND PEPPER TO TASTE
EMPANADA DOUGH (STORE-BOUGHT OR HOMEMADE)
1 EGG, BEATEN

RECIPE:

1. In a skillet, cook ground beef with onions and garlic until browned.
2. Add cumin, salt, and pepper. Mix well.
3. Preheat oven to 400°F (200°C).
4. Roll out empanada dough and cut into circles.
5. Place a spoonful of the beef mixture in the center of each circle.
6. Fold dough over the filling and seal the edges.
7. Brush the tops with beaten egg.
8. Bake for 20-25 minutes until golden.

Fun Fact: Empanadas are believed to have originated in Spain, but each Latin American country has its own unique spin on the dish.

Chef Insights: You can also use chicken, cheese, or vegetables as the filling. Crimping the edges with a fork not only seals the empanadas but also gives them a decorative finish.

CUBANO SANDWICH

INGREDIENTS:

1 LOAF CUBAN BREAD
1/2 LB SLICED ROAST PORK
1/2 LB SLICED HAM
1/2 LB SWISS CHEESE
DILL PICKLES, SLICED
MUSTARD
BUTTER FOR SPREADING

RECIPE:

1. Preheat a griddle or panini press.
2. Slice the Cuban bread into sandwich-length pieces and cut them open.
3. Layer ham, roast pork, Swiss cheese, and pickles on one side of the bread.
4. Spread mustard on the other side.
5. Close the sandwiches and butter the outer surfaces.
6. Grill on the preheated griddle until the cheese is melted and the bread is crisp.

Fun Fact: Despite its name, the Cubano sandwich was actually invented in Florida by Cuban immigrants.

Chef Insights: Using a panini press gives you that authentic, pressed texture, but a skillet will work too. The roast pork is what sets this apart; marinate it well for best results.

Latin cuisine

AREPAS

INGREDIENTS:

2 CUPS MASAREPA (PRE-COOKED CORNMEAL)
2 CUPS WARM WATER
1 TSP SALT
1 TBSP VEGETABLE OIL

RECIPE:

1. In a bowl, mix masarepa, warm water, and salt until a dough forms.
2. Let rest for 5 minutes.
3. Shape into small, thick patties.
4. Heat oil in a skillet and cook arepas until golden brown on each side.

Fun Fact: Arepas are a staple in both Venezuela and Colombia, and each country claims them as their own!

Chef Insights: Masarepa is essential for the authentic taste and texture; don't substitute with regular cornmeal. You can stuff arepas with anything from cheese and ham to more elaborate fillings like Reina Pepiada.

TAMALES

INGREDIENTS:

2 CUPS MASA HARINA
1 CUP CHICKEN BROTH
1 TSP BAKING POWDER
1/2 CUP LARD OR SHORTENING
2 CUPS FILLING (COOKED SHREDDED CHICKEN, BEEF, OR VEGETABLES)
CORN HUSKS, SOAKED IN HOT WATER

RECIPE:

1. In a mixing bowl, combine masa harina, baking powder, and salt.
2. Add chicken broth and lard. Mix until smooth.
3. Spread a small amount of masa mixture onto a soaked corn husk.
4. Add a tablespoon of your chosen filling.
5. Fold the sides of the husk in, then fold up the bottom.
6. Steam the tamales for about 1-1.5 hours.

Fun Fact: Tamales have been made for thousands of years, and they were even used as portable food for Aztec, Maya, and Inca warriors.

Chef Insights: Soaking the corn husks makes them more pliable and easier to fold. You can add salsas, cheeses, or herbs to your filling for added flavor.

Latin cuisine

CHURROS

INGREDIENTS:

1 CUP WATER
2 TBSP SUGAR
1/2 TSP SALT
2 TBSP VEGETABLE OIL
1 CUP ALL-PURPOSE FLOUR
OIL FOR FRYING
SUGAR AND CINNAMON FOR DUSTING

RECIPE:

1. Bring water, sugar, salt, and 2 tbsp vegetable oil to a boil.
2. Remove from heat and stir in flour until a ball forms.
3. Heat oil for frying to 375°F (190°C).
4. Pipe strips of dough into hot oil using a pastry bag with a star nozzle.
5. Fry until golden, drain, and dust with sugar and cinnamon.

Fun Fact: While churros are popular in Latin America, they actually originated in Spain.

Chef Insights: A star nozzle will give your churros that traditional ridged surface, which helps to hold the sugar. Make sure your oil is at the correct temperature to avoid soggy churros.

CHIMICHURRI

INGREDIENTS:

1 CUP FRESH PARSLEY, FINELY CHOPPED
4 CLOVES GARLIC, MINCED
1/2 CUP OLIVE OIL
2 TABLESPOONS RED WINE VINEGAR
1 TEASPOON SALT
1/4 TEASPOON PEPPER
1/4 TEASPOON RED PEPPER FLAKES

RECIPE:

1. Combine parsley, garlic, olive oil, red wine vinegar, salt, pepper, and red pepper flakes in a bowl.
2. Mix well until fully combined.
3. Let it sit for at least 30 minutes to allow the flavors to meld.
4. Serve as a dipping sauce or marinade.

Fun Fact: Chimichurri is said to have been named after Jimmy McCurry, an Irishman who fought in the Argentine War of Independence. The name was then "nativized" into Spanish as 'chimichurri'.

Chef Insights: Use a food processor for a smoother sauce, but hand chopping ingredients brings a rustic touch. It tastes even better if you let it sit in the fridge overnight!

Latin cuisine

PUPUSAS

INGREDIENTS:

2 CUPS MASA HARINA
1 1/4 CUPS WARM WATER
1 CUP GRATED CHEESE (QUESO DURO OR MOZZARELLA)
1 CUP COOKED REFRIED BEANS

RECIPE:

1. Mix masa harina and warm water to form a dough.
2. Divide the dough into small balls.
3. Flatten each ball and add a tablespoon of cheese and refried beans.
4. Fold the dough over the filling and seal.
5. Flatten gently to make a disc shape.
6. Cook on a hot griddle until both sides are golden.

Fun Fact: Pupusas were created by the Pipil tribes of El Salvador, possibly as far back as 2000 years ago.

Chef Insights: You can fill pupusas with various ingredients like pork, jalapeños, or even zucchini. Don't over-stuff; the masa needs to be able to fully seal the filling inside.

MOLE

INGREDIENTS:

1 TABLESPOON VEGETABLE OIL
1 ONION, CHOPPED
4 CLOVES GARLIC, MINCED
2 TEASPOONS CUMIN
1 TEASPOON CINNAMON
1/2 CUP UNSWEETENED COCOA POWDER
1 CAN (14 OZ) CRUSHED TOMATOES
2 CUPS CHICKEN OR VEGETABLE BROTH
4 DRIED ANCHO CHILIES, SOAKED AND CHOPPED
1/4 CUP ALMONDS OR PEANUTS, CRUSHED
1 TEASPOON SALT

RECIPE:

1. In a saucepan, sauté onion and garlic in vegetable oil until soft.
2. Add cumin, cinnamon, and cocoa powder, stir to combine.
3. Add crushed tomatoes, broth, ancho chilies, nuts, and salt.
4. Simmer on low heat for 30 minutes.
5. Blend until smooth.
6. Serve over chicken, turkey, or vegetables.

Fun Fact: The word "mole" originates from the Nahuatl word "mōlli," which means "sauce" or "concoction." Mole can include over 20 ingredients and can take a full day to prepare in its most traditional form.

Chef Insights: Don't rush the simmering; it's essential for the flavors to meld. If you're feeling adventurous, try adding some chocolate to enhance the depth of flavors.

Latin cuisine

FEIJOADA

INGREDIENTS:

**1 LB BLACK BEANS
4 CUPS WATER
1 LB PORK SHOULDER, CUT INTO CHUNKS
1 LB CHORIZO SAUSAGES, CUT INTO CHUNKS
1 LB BEEF STEW MEAT, CUT INTO CHUNKS
1 ONION, CHOPPED
4 CLOVES GARLIC, MINCED
2 BAY LEAVES
SALT AND PEPPER TO TASTE**

RECIPE:

1. Soak black beans overnight in water.
2. In a large pot, add soaked beans, pork shoulder, chorizo, beef, onion, garlic, and bay leaves.
3. Add water to cover the ingredients.
4. Bring to a boil, then reduce heat and simmer for about 2 hours.
5. Season with salt and pepper to taste.
6. Serve with rice and orange slices.

Fun Fact: Feijoada is often considered the national dish of Brazil. It's traditionally eaten on weekends with family and friends.

Chef Insights: This dish is often served with farofa (toasted cassava flour) and collard greens. Feel free to vary the meats according to what you have; it's a very forgiving dish!

Festive and Holiday

Festive and Holiday

ROAST TURKEY

INGREDIENTS:

1 (12-14 LBS) WHOLE TURKEY,
THAWED
1 ONION, QUARTERED
1 LEMON, HALVED

4 SPRIGS FRESH THYME
4 SPRIGS FRESH ROSEMARY
1/2 CUP UNSALTED BUTTER, MELTED
SALT AND PEPPER TO TASTE

RECIPE:

1. Preheat the oven to 325°F (163°C).
2. Remove giblets and neck from the turkey and rinse it under cold water
3. Pat the turkey dry with paper towels.
4. Stuff the turkey cavity with the onion, lemon, thyme, and rosemary.
5. Brush the turkey with melted butter, and season with salt and pepper.
6. Place the turkey in a roasting pan.
7. Roast for about 15 minutes per pound or until the internal temperature reaches 165°F (74°C).
8. Rest for 20 minutes before carving.

Fun Fact: the tradition of eating turkey on Thanksgiving started in the 17th century. However, it wasn't until the 1940s that turkey became synonymous with Thanksgiving.

Chef Insights: For a moist and flavorful turkey, consider brining it a day before cooking. Brining allows the turkey to absorb the flavors and helps it retain moisture during roasting.

GLAZED HAM

INGREDIENTS:

1 (8-10 LBS) BONE-IN HAM
1 CUP BROWN SUGAR
1/2 CUP HONEY
1/4 CUP DIJON MUSTARD
1/4 CUP PINEAPPLE JUICE

RECIPE:

1. Preheat the oven to 350°F (175°C).
2. Score the surface of the ham in a diamond pattern.
3. Place the ham in a roasting pan and cover with foil.
4. Roast for 1 hour.
5. In a saucepan, combine brown sugar, honey, mustard, and pineapple juice. Simmer until it forms a thick glaze.
6. Brush the glaze over the ham.
7. Return to the oven and bake for an additional 30-45 minutes, basting occasionally.
8. Remove from oven and let it rest before slicing.

Fun Fact: Ham has been a festive dish for centuries, dating back to at least the Roman times. They considered it a "special occasion" meat due to its expense and the labor needed for its preparation and cooking.

Chef Insights: Using a bone-in ham provides more flavor. Also, the bone can be saved for soup or stocks, maximizing the value of your purchase.

Festive and Holiday

PUMPKIN PIE

INGREDIENTS:

1 (9-INCH) UNBAKED PIE CRUST
2 CUPS CANNED PUMPKIN PUREE
1 CUP HEAVY CREAM
2/3 CUP GRANULATED SUGAR
2 EGGS

1 TEASPOON CINNAMON
1/2 TEASPOON NUTMEG
1/4 TEASPOON GINGER
1/4 TEASPOON CLOVES
1/4 TEASPOON SALT

RECIPE:

1. Preheat the oven to 425°F (220°C).
2. In a bowl, combine pumpkin puree, heavy cream, sugar, eggs, and spices.
3. Pour the mixture into the pie crust.
4. Bake for 15 minutes, then reduce the temperature to 350°F (175°C).
5. Continue baking for 35-45 minutes, or until a knife inserted into the center comes out clean.
6. Let the pie cool before serving.

Fun Fact: Pumpkin pies were not at the original Thanksgiving feast but were integrated into the holiday tradition in the early 18th century as pumpkin was abundant and easy to store.

Chef Insights: For a unique twist, try adding a tablespoon of bourbon to your pumpkin pie filling. It gives an extra layer of warmth and complexity.

FRUITCAKE

INGREDIENTS:

1 CUP DRIED CHERRIES	4 LARGE EGGS
1 CUP DRIED APRICOTS, CHOPPED	1 CUP ALL-PURPOSE FLOUR
1 CUP RAISINS	1/2 TEASPOON GROUND CINNAMON
1 CUP MIXED PEEL	1/4 TEASPOON GROUND NUTMEG
1 CUP UNSALTED BUTTER, SOFTENED	1/4 CUP BRANDY OR RUM, PLUS
1 CUP BROWN SUGAR	MORE FOR SOAKING

RECIPE:

1. Preheat the oven to 300°F (150°C). Grease and line a 9-inch round cake pan.
2. In a bowl, mix together the dried fruits.
3. In another bowl, cream the butter and sugar until light and fluffy.
4. Add the eggs one at a time, beating well after each addition.
5. Sift in the flour and spices, and fold into the batter.
6. Add the mixed dried fruits and brandy, mixing until combined.
7. Pour the batter into the prepared cake pan and smooth the top.
8. Bake for 2-3 hours or until a toothpick comes out clean.
9. Once cool, brush with more brandy and wrap in parchment paper to age for at least a few days before serving.

Fun Fact: Fruitcake has a long shelf life and can be stored for months if properly preserved. In fact, in some families, it is saved and eaten a year later to celebrate a special occasion.

Chef Insights: If you find traditional fruitcake too dense, consider folding in some beaten egg whites before baking. This lightens the texture without compromising the rich flavors.

Festive and Holiday

HOLIDAY COOKIES

INGREDIENTS:

3 CUPS ALL-PURPOSE FLOUR
1 1/2 TEASPOONS BAKING POWDER
1/2 TEASPOON SALT
1 CUP UNSALTED BUTTER, SOFTENED
1 CUP SUGAR

1 LARGE EGG
1 TEASPOON VANILLA EXTRACT
VARIOUS COOKIE CUTTERS, ICING,
AND SPRINKLES FOR DECORATION

RECIPE:

1. Preheat the oven to 350°F (175°C). Line a cookie sheet with parchment paper.
2. Whisk together flour, baking powder, and salt in a bowl.
3. In another bowl, cream the butter and sugar until fluffy.
4. Add the egg and vanilla extract, mixing well.
5. Gradually add the dry ingredients to the wet ingredients, mixing until a dough forms.
6. Roll out the dough and cut out cookies using cookie cutters.
7. Place cookies on the cookie sheet and bake for 8-12 minutes until lightly golden.
8. Allow cookies to cool before adding icing and sprinkles.

Fun Fact: The tradition of making holiday cookies dates back to Medieval Europe. The recipes were a symbol of good fortune and were often used as offerings to gods or decorations for the tree.

Chef Insights: When making cookies, chilling the dough before rolling and cutting can make it easier to handle and also improve the texture and flavor of the baked cookies.

EGGNOG

INGREDIENTS:

4 CUPS WHOLE MILK
1 CUP HEAVY CREAM
1/2 CUP SUGAR
6 LARGE EGG YOLKS

1 TEASPOON GROUND NUTMEG
1 TEASPOON VANILLA EXTRACT
1/2 CUP RUM OR BOURBON
(OPTIONAL)

RECIPE:

1. In a saucepan, heat milk, cream, and half of the sugar until hot but not boiling.
2. In a bowl, whisk the egg yolks with the remaining sugar until well combined.
3. Slowly add the hot milk mixture to the egg yolks while whisking constantly.
4. Return the mixture to the saucepan and heat on low, stirring continuously until it thickens.
5. Remove from heat and add nutmeg, vanilla, and alcohol if using.
6. Chill before serving.

Fun Fact: Eggnog is believed to have originated from the medieval British drink "posset," a warm ale punch with eggs and figs.

Chef Insights: If you're nervous about using raw eggs, you can use pasteurized eggs or cook the egg-milk mixture to at least 160°F (71°C) to ensure it's food-safe.

Festive and Holiday

LATKES

INGREDIENTS:

4 LARGE RUSSET POTATOES, PEELED AND GRATED
1 MEDIUM ONION, GRATED
2 LARGE EGGS, BEATEN
1/4 CUP ALL-PURPOSE FLOUR
SALT AND PEPPER TO TASTE
VEGETABLE OIL FOR FRYING

RECIPE:

1. In a bowl, combine the grated potatoes and onions.
2. Add eggs, flour, salt, and pepper, and mix well.
3. Heat oil in a skillet over medium-high heat.
4. Spoon portions of the potato mixture into the hot oil, flattening them into pancakes.
5. Fry until golden brown on each side.
6. Drain on paper towels and serve hot.

Fun Fact: Latkes are traditionally eaten during Hanukkah to commemorate the miracle of the oil that burned for eight days.

Chef Insights: The key to crispy latkes is removing as much moisture as possible from the grated potatoes. Consider using a clean kitchen towel to wring out the water.

HOT CROSS BUNS

INGREDIENTS:

4 CUPS ALL-PURPOSE FLOUR
1/2 CUP SUGAR
1 PACKAGE (2 1/4 TSP) ACTIVE DRY YEAST
1/2 TEASPOON SALT
1 TEASPOON GROUND CINNAMON
1/2 TEASPOON GROUND NUTMEG

1 CUP WARM MILK
1/2 CUP MELTED BUTTER
2 LARGE EGGS
1 CUP RAISINS OR CURRANTS
FOR THE CROSS: 1/4 CUP FLOUR MIXED WITH WATER TO MAKE A THICK PASTE

RECIPE:

1. In a large bowl, mix flour, sugar, yeast, salt, cinnamon, and nutmeg.
2. Add warm milk, melted butter, and eggs. Mix until a dough forms.
3. Knead in raisins or currants.
4. Let the dough rise for 1 hour or until doubled in size.
5. Divide the dough into 12 equal parts and shape into buns.
6. Pipe the flour paste to form crosses on each bun.
7. Bake at 375°F (190°C) for 20-25 minutes, or until golden brown.

Fun Fact: Hot Cross Buns are traditionally eaten on Good Friday, and they have been associated with various myths and superstitions throughout history.

Chef Insights: Feel free to get creative with the fillings; chocolate chips or dried cranberries can also make delightful alternatives.

Festive and Holiday

CORNED BEEF AND CABBAGE

INGREDIENTS:

3-4 LBS CORNED BEEF BRISKET
1 ONION, QUARTERED
4 CLOVES GARLIC, CRUSHED
1 TEASPOON BLACK PEPPERCORNS
4 CUPS BEEF BROTH

1 HEAD OF CABBAGE, CUT INTO
WEDGES
4-5 MEDIUM POTATOES, QUARTERED
4 CARROTS, CUT INTO CHUNKS

RECIPE:

1. Place corned beef in a large pot with onion, garlic, and peppercorns.
2. Cover with beef broth and bring to a boil.
3. Reduce heat and simmer for 3 hours or until tender.
4. Add cabbage, potatoes, and carrots during the last 30 minutes of cooking.
5. Slice corned beef against the grain and serve with vegetables.

Fun Fact: Corned Beef and Cabbage is more of an Irish-American tradition than an Irish one, gaining popularity among Irish immigrants in the United States.

Chef Insights: If your corned beef is pre-brined with spices, you can skip the peppercorns for a milder flavor.

BEEF WELLINGTON

INGREDIENTS:

2-3 LB BEEF TENDERLOIN, TRIMMED
2 TBSP OLIVE OIL
SALT AND PEPPER, TO SEASON
8 SLICES PARMA HAM
2 CUPS MUSHROOMS, FINELY
CHOPPED (BUTTON OR CREMINI)
2 CLOVES GARLIC, MINCED

1 SHALLOT, FINELY CHOPPED
1/4 CUP DRY WHITE WINE
1 TBSP FRESH THYME LEAVES
2 TBSP DIJON MUSTARD
1 PACKAGE PUFF PASTRY, THAWED
1 EGG, BEATEN

RECIPE:

1. Preheat the oven to 400°F (200°C).
2. Season the beef tenderloin with salt and pepper. Heat olive oil in a skillet over high heat, and sear the beef on all sides until browned. Remove and let cool.
3. In the same skillet, add garlic, shallots, and mushrooms. Sauté until the mushrooms release their moisture. Add thyme and white wine, cooking until the mixture becomes a thick paste. Remove from heat and let cool.
4. Lay out the Parma ham slices on a sheet of cling film, slightly overlapping. Spread the mushroom mixture over the ham.
5. Brush the beef tenderloin with Dijon mustard, then roll it up in the Parma ham and mushroom layer using the cling film to help you. Chill in the fridge for 15 minutes.
6. Roll out the puff pastry on a floured surface. Unwrap the beef from the cling film and place it in the center of the pastry. Fold the pastry over the beef and seal the edges.

Festive and Holiday

7. Place the wrapped beef on a baking sheet, seam-side down. Brush with beaten egg.
8. Bake for 25-30 minutes, or until the pastry is golden brown.
9. Let the Beef Wellington rest for 10 minutes before slicing.

Fun Fact: Beef Wellington is named after the Duke of Wellington, Arthur Wellesley, though it's unclear if he ever ate the dish or if it was just a patriotic naming.

Chef Insights: It's crucial to let the beef rest before slicing to retain its juicy interior. Also, make sure your mushroom mixture is as dry as possible; this will help keep the pastry crisp.

Quick and Easy

Quick & Easy

CHICKEN STIR-FRY

INGREDIENTS:

1 LB CHICKEN BREAST, THINLY SLICED
2 CUPS MIXED VEGETABLES (BELL PEPPERS, CARROTS, BROCCOLI)
3 CLOVES GARLIC, MINCED
1 TBSP GINGER, GRATED
1/4 CUP SOY SAUCE
2 TBSP SESAME OIL
SALT AND PEPPER, TO TASTE

RECIPE:

1. Heat a wok or large skillet over high heat and add sesame oil.
2. Add garlic and ginger, stirring for about 30 seconds.
3. Add chicken slices and stir-fry until they're no longer pink.
4. Add mixed vegetables and stir-fry for another 3-4 minutes.
5. Add soy sauce and mix well. Season with salt and pepper.
6. Serve immediately over steamed rice.

Fun Fact: Stir-frying is a cooking technique originally from China, and it's designed to prepare food quickly and without much oil, making it a healthier option.

Chef Insights: Always prepare all your ingredients before heating the wok. Stir-frying is a fast process, and you don't want to be caught chopping veggies while your garlic is burning.

CALIFORNIA BLT

INGREDIENTS:

4 SLICES SOURDOUGH BREAD
4 SLICES BACON
2 LETTUCE LEAVES
1 LARGE TOMATO, SLICED
1 AVOCADO, SLICED
2 TBSP MAYONNAISE
SALT AND PEPPER, TO TASTE

RECIPE:

1. Cook bacon slices in a skillet until crispy. Drain on paper towels.
2. Toast the sourdough bread.
3. Spread mayonnaise on one side of each bread slice.
4. Layer bacon, lettuce, tomato, and avocado slices on one bread slice, and season with salt and pepper.
5. Top with the second slice of bread.
6. Repeat to make the second sandwich.

Fun Fact: The BLT likely has its origins from tea sandwiches that were popular with the British upper class in the 18th century.

Chef Insights: Using ripe avocados and crispy, quality bacon makes all the difference. Also, toasting the bread helps it hold up against the moist ingredients.

APPLE TARTS

INGREDIENTS:

1 SHEET PUFF PASTRY, THAWED
2 LARGE APPLES, THINLY SLICED
1/4 CUP BROWN SUGAR
1 TSP CINNAMON
1 TBSP LEMON JUICE
1 EGG, BEATEN (FOR EGG WASH)

RECIPE:

1. Preheat oven to 375°F (190°C).
2. Roll out the puff pastry and cut into 4 rectangles.
3. In a bowl, mix apple slices, brown sugar, cinnamon, and lemon juice.
4. Arrange apple slices on each pastry rectangle.
5. Brush the edges with egg wash.
6. Bake for 18-20 minutes or until the pastry is golden.
7. Serve warm.

Fun Fact: The apple tart is a simplified version of the French 'Tarte Tatin,' a caramelized upside-down tart.

Chef Insights: Always make sure your puff pastry is cold but not frozen for best results; this will give you that crisp, flaky texture.

GARLIC MUSHROOM

INGREDIENTS:

1 LB BUTTON MUSHROOMS
4 CLOVES GARLIC, MINCED
1/4 CUP WHITE WINE
1/4 CUP BUTTER
SALT AND PEPPER, TO TASTE
CHOPPED PARSLEY, FOR GARNISH

RECIPE:

1. In a skillet, melt butter over medium heat.
2. Add garlic and sauté until fragrant.
3. Add mushrooms and cook until they start to soften.
4. Pour in white wine and allow it to reduce by half.
5. Season with salt and pepper.
6. Garnish with chopped parsley before serving.

Fun Fact: Mushrooms are incredibly versatile and are used in various cuisines. They are actually closer to animals than plants in a biological sense!

Chef Insights: Use a good quality white wine that you'd drink; the flavor will concentrate as it cooks.

Quick & Easy

SHEET PAN FAJITAS

INGREDIENTS:

2 LBS CHICKEN BREASTS, THINLY SLICED
3 BELL PEPPERS, THINLY SLICED
1 LARGE ONION, THINLY SLICED
2 TBSP OLIVE OIL
1 PACKET FAJITA SEASONING
JUICE OF 1 LIME
TORTILLAS, FOR SERVING

RECIPE:

1. Preheat oven to 400°F (200°C).
2. On a large sheet pan, combine chicken, bell peppers, and onions.
3. Drizzle with olive oil and sprinkle fajita seasoning. Mix well.
4. Bake for 20-25 minutes, stirring halfway through.
5. Squeeze lime juice over the cooked ingredients.
6. Serve with tortillas.

Fun Fact: Fajitas were originally made from skirt steak, a throwaway cut of beef, by Mexican ranch workers along the Texas-Mexico border.

Chef Insights: Don't overcrowd the sheet pan. This allows for better heat circulation, ensuring all ingredients cook evenly.

Beyond Instant Noodles. 200 Quick & Easy College Recipes

GRILLED CHEESE SANDWICH

INGREDIENTS:

4 SLICES OF BREAD
4 SLICES OF CHEDDAR CHEESE
2 TBSP BUTTER, SOFTENED

RECIPE:

1. Butter one side of each slice of bread.
2. Place a slice of cheese between two slices of bread, butter side out.
3. In a skillet over medium heat, cook until each side is golden brown and cheese is melted.
4. Serve immediately.

Fun Fact: The grilled cheese sandwich dates back to Roman times, but the modern version we know came to be in the 1920s with the invention of sliced bread and processed cheese.

Chef Insights: For a rich, crispy texture, try using a combination of butter and a touch of mayonnaise on the bread before grilling.

Quick & Easy

CHOCOLATE MOUSSE

INGREDIENTS:

200G DARK CHOCOLATE, CHOPPED
3 LARGE EGGS
1/4 CUP SUGAR
1 CUP HEAVY CREAM

RECIPE:

1. Melt the chocolate in a double boiler and let it cool slightly.
2. Whip the heavy cream until stiff peaks form. Set aside.
3. In another bowl, beat the eggs and sugar until light and fluffy.
4. Fold the melted chocolate into the egg mixture.
5. Gently fold in the whipped cream until well combined.
6. Divide into serving cups and chill for at least 2 hours.

Fun Fact: The word "mousse" in French means "foam," which aptly describes the dish's light, airy texture.

Chef Insights: For an extra kick, you can add a splash of liqueur like Grand Marnier to the chocolate mixture. Just make sure to adjust the sugar accordingly.

BREAKFAST BURRITO

INGREDIENTS:

4 LARGE EGGS
1/4 CUP MILK
SALT AND PEPPER TO TASTE
1 CUP COOKED AND CRUMBLED BREAKFAST SAUSAGE
1 CUP SHREDDED CHEDDAR CHEESE
4 LARGE FLOUR TORTILLAS

RECIPE:

1. Whisk together eggs, milk, salt, and pepper.
2. Cook the egg mixture in a non-stick skillet over medium heat, stirring occasionally.
3. Warm the tortillas in a dry skillet or microwave.
4. Assemble the burritos: Lay out a tortilla, then add a scoop of scrambled eggs, crumbled sausage, and a sprinkle of cheese.
5. Fold the sides in and roll up the tortilla to form a burrito.
6. Serve immediately or wrap in foil for on-the-go.

Fun Fact: Breakfast burritos originated in the Southwestern United States but have gained popularity all over due to their convenience and adaptability.

Chef Insights: If you want to make these ahead, they freeze really well. Just wrap each burrito tightly in aluminum foil and freeze. Reheat in the oven or microwave when ready to eat.

Quick & Easy

MASON JAR SALAD

INGREDIENTS:

1/4 CUP BALSAMIC VINAIGRETTE
1 CUP CHERRY TOMATOES, HALVED
1 CUP COOKED QUINOA
1 CUP DICED CUCUMBER
1 CUP BABY SPINACH
1/2 CUP CRUMBLED FETA CHEESE

RECIPE:

1. Start with the balsamic vinaigrette at the bottom of the Mason jar.
2. Layer cherry tomatoes next, followed by quinoa.
3. Add the cucumber, then the baby spinach.
4. Finish with a layer of crumbled feta cheese.
5. Seal the jar tightly and refrigerate until ready to eat. Shake well before eating.

Fun Fact: The Mason jar was invented in 1858 by John Landis Mason, and it's a brilliant vessel for storing salads because it keeps the wet and dry ingredients separate until you're ready to eat.

Chef Insights: Layering is key here. Always start with the dressing at the bottom and end with the leafy greens at the top to keep everything fresh and crisp.

MICROWAVE MUG CAKE

INGREDIENTS:

4 TBSP ALL-PURPOSE FLOUR
2 TBSP SUGAR
2 TBSP COCOA POWDER
3 TBSP MILK
2 TBSP VEGETABLE OIL
1/4 TSP VANILLA EXTRACT

RECIPE:

1. In a microwave-safe mug, mix the flour, sugar, and cocoa powder.
2. Add the milk, vegetable oil, and vanilla extract. Mix until smooth.
3. Microwave on high for about 90 seconds or until the cake has risen and is set in the middle.
4. Let it cool for a couple of minutes before eating.

Fun Fact: Microwave cooking was discovered accidentally when Percy Spencer, an American engineer, stood next to a radar set and noticed a chocolate bar in his pocket had melted.

Chef Insights: The cooking time can vary depending on your microwave's wattage, so keep an eye on the cake to prevent it from overflowing or drying out.

Thank you!

So, we went a little crazy and put together this monster cookbook with 200 recipes from all over the world. Why? Because we remember those days of being stuck between the same old cafeteria food and instant noodles. Dark times, my friends.

Parents, if you're reading this - your kids are gonna think you're the coolest for hooking them up. Students, get ready to become the most popular person on your floor. (Pro tip: Food is the ultimate friend-maker.)

If this book saves you from another night of sad microwave meals, spread the love! Drop a review on Amazon. Your stories might just inspire another poor soul to put down the instant ramen and pick up a spatula.

Now go forth and cook something awesome! Your taste buds (and future self) will thank you.

You can use this QR code to submit your review

More books available on Amazon.com

- **200 Jobs Explained: The Ultimate Career Guide.** Discover the career of your dreams with 200 career profiles to explore

- **500 Careers and Salaries: The Job Seeker's Atlas.** Salaries and Roles Across Industries

- **"Famous in STEM" collection:**

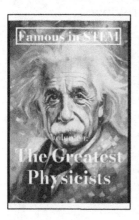

- 101 Emotions Explained: The Ultimate Guide to Recognize and Understand Our Feelings for Greater Self-Awareness and Emotional Well-Being

- "Excel Tips And Tricks: Answers The Top Excel Questions On The Internet"

Made in United States
North Haven, CT
10 November 2024

60109962R00134